1996

THE PHILOSOPHY OF RIGHT

*****

Rights in God's Church

ANTONIO ROSMINI

THE PHILOSOPHY OF RIGHT

Volume 4

Rights in God's Church

Translated by
DENIS CLEARY
and
TERENCE WATSON

ROSMINI HOUSE
DURHAM

Translated from
Filosofia del Diritto
Vol. 2, Intra, 1865

Typeset by Rosmini House, Durham
Printed by Bell & Bain Limited, Glasgow

ISBN 1 899093 10 9

Note

Square brackets [ ] indicate notes or additions by the translators.

References to this and other works of Rosmini are given by paragraph number unless otherwise stated.

Abbreviations used for Rosmini's quoted works are:

AMS: *Anthropology as an Aid to Moral Science*
CE: *Certainty*
ER: *The Essence of Right,* vol. 1 of *The Philosophy of Right*
OT: *The Origin of Thought*
PE: *Principles of Ethics*
RI: *Rights of the Individual,* vol. 2 of *The Philosophy of Right*
SP: *Society and its Purpose,* vol. 2 of *The Phiilosophy of Politics*

Foreword

The three preceding volumes of the English translation of Rosmini's *The Philosophy of Right* have dealt with the essence of right (vol. 1), individual rights (vol. 2) and the principles underlying social right (vol. 3). In the present work and the two following volumes, Rosmini undertakes to apply these principles to the three societies necessary for 'the perfect organisation of mankind', theocratic, domestic and civil society, all of which are common to the human race.

Rights in God's Church is an examination of the society formed between God and human beings. The society to which Rosmini refers is theocratic in the strict sense, that is, ruled *de facto* and *de jure* by God himself. Although the rulers on earth of this society will necessarily be the representatives of God, the society itself is not theocratic in the debased sense of a *civil* society governed by priests or some kind of hierarchy where the interests served are more likely to be those of the pseudo-rulers than of God. It is a society in which men and women look to God as their Creator on the level of nature or, as in Christianity, share in the life of the Creator-God, Father, Son and Holy Spirit, through the redemption wrought by Jesus Christ, the incarnate Son of God and Word made flesh, while accepting the visible society established by Christ to continue his work on earth.

It is clear that attempting to deal with such a subject under the general heading 'philosophy of Right' raises immediate problems. First, the separation of religion from philosophical thinking, a process accelerated and completed by the Enlightenment, is so endemic in intellectual circles that the very notion of theocratic society in any sense is dismissed out of hand. Second, it is difficult to imagine how philosophy can approach the question of right(s) appertaining to and exercised in religion, which not only demands the service due to God on a purely natural level but also at a supernatural level, where its foundation depends on God's revelation, not on human conclusions.

Third, the practical atheism hidden under the fripperies that to a great extent pass for Christianity in Western society is not prepared to tolerate the presence in its midst of a Church with rights to existence, propagation and development.

Each of these problems is faced squarely by Rosmini in the treatise, to which the reader must be referred. But recognition of these problems, and the consequent difficulty experienced by minds totally unaccustomed to such an approach, may be tempered in general by a glance at the indifferent state of any domestic and civil society in which religious society plays no practical part. It is a fact, not a propagandistic assertion, that the withdrawal of interest in the things of God has gone hand in hand with the progressive disintegration of domestic and civil society in nations under the influence of Western 'civilisation'. This alone should make us wary of rejecting out of hand any attempt at re-instating religious society as the foundation on which all other societies must rest.

There are, moreover, highly positive reasons for a sympathetic review of Rosmini's position. Many of these will be obvious to adherents of religion and need not be mentioned here. One, however, deserves emphasis. Only religious society has as its end the supreme, unique, true and final good of mankind. The aim of every other, lesser society is only a part of this end and, as such, necessarily fragmented. No other society, therefore, is capable of drawing the human race into one, great family. Without religion, there can be no unity amongst mankind; with religion, mankind may not at any given moment achieve the unity to which it is called — there will always be anti-religious factions amongst humankind — but it will constantly march towards it. Hope will never be abandoned.

DENIS CLEARY
TERENCE WATSON

Durham,
June, 1995

Contents

SECTION TWO

GOVERNMENTAL RIGHT IN THEOCRATIC SOCIETY

SECTION THREE

COMMUNAL RIGHT IN PERFECT THEOCRATIC SOCIETY

SOCIAL RIGHT

SPECIAL-SOCIAL RIGHT

Part 1

RIGHT IN THEOCRATIC SOCIETY

> Jurisprudence is knowledge of DIVINE and HUMAN things, the verdict about what is just and unjust
>
> *(Instit.* 1. 1: 2)

INTRODUCTION

477. All the kinds of society listed and classified in *Universal Social Right*, (cf. 50–141) are subject to universal Right, outlined rather than studied in the preceding book; each is also regulated by its own special Right.

478. This Right is partly *rational*, partly *conventional*.

479. The rational part is deduced by reasoning from the end and nature of the society under consideration; it is the outcome of *jural reason*.

480. The *conventional* part consists in the conventions agreed by individuals who form societies.

481. The conventional part is an element of *applied, or realised Right*, because it results from *real* facts, such as conventions, and not from simple possibilities. The *rational* part, on the other hand, belongs to *pure Right*. The particular societies which it examines are not considered in their subsistent reality, but as possibilities; pure Right considers the *essence* of these societies, without investigating whether they can actually be found. Information about their formation by mankind has no bearing on the aim of the study.

482. The parts of rational Right, in so far as it governs particular societies, correspond to the number of societies it studies. However, it is obvious that listing these would require endless work, and that studying the Right of each would be useless. We must restrict our investigations, and the best way of doing this is perhaps by limiting our study in this and the following two books to the treatment of *special-social Right*.

483. Many particular societies can help the individuals who form them, and other persons, without being necessary for

mankind. Some, however, are necessary for the well-being and progress of the human family. Mankind, this multitude of individuals, could not exist on earth nor develop towards its earthly perfection and immortal destiny unless it were ordered and bound together in accord with the stimuli provided by nature, moral relationships, and needs. Mankind requires organisation, and some societies are necessary because they are conditions and indeed constitutive parts of this organisation. Special-social Right cannot avoid dealing with these subjects to which our study will be confined. The next three books, therefore, will be devoted exclusively to the *Right of societies necessary for the perfect organisation of mankind*, without reference to other human associations.

484. Which are the societies indispensable for the perfect organisation of mankind?

485. The three following: theocratic, domestic and civil society.

486. This book deals with theocratic society; the other two with domestic and civil society.

I know, of course, that the phrase, 'theocratic society', grates on many people, and I could easily have avoided it if I had wanted to attract my readers with something other than the truth. But I want to reason with my contemporaries; flattering them would do me no good. The presence of reasonable human beings in our modern world comforts and encourages me. I want to communicate with people prepared to reason about everything, including their own opinions, which they are ready to abandon if necessary. I want to speak to decent people prepared to listen to the end of an argument quietly reasoned in good faith. But I have to add that I am addressing all men and women because I know that all possess reason, even those who choke on the first word they hear opposed to their own feelings and passions. There is no obligation to read the book; it can be opened and closed at will. Books are always courteous: they never talk to those who prefer not to listen; they keep silence when not questioned. But I do hope to obtain a hearing from readers inspired by noble, religious considerations, and struck by mankind's need for a perfect, divine morality if it is to attain salvation. I hope they will pay suitable attention to whatever in this volume is helpful and important for mankind, and take pity on anything which is or seems useless. Attention and criticism are in fact at home in such persons who never close the door on the truth, even if human prejudices obscure their goodness and wisdom.

487. On the other hand, the majority of those who detest the word 'theocracy' take it in a sense different from that in which it is used here. They are afraid that people may want to profit unjustly in human affairs under cover of divine matters. But there are no grounds for suspecting that this book is intended to defend or teach this detestable abuse of divine things. Not a shadow of such sacrilege can be detected in what has been written. On the contrary, the dictates of decency, justice and religion have willingly been emphasised in order to free human society from such extreme danger which, however, cannot be avoided when injustice, irreligion or impiety set out to subvert the city of the Lord by what they consider a work of highest justice (although there is no chance that evil enterprises will further human happiness). Every decent person needs to be persuaded that the rights of individuals, of civil society, and of rulers are much more effectively guaranteed by the faithful fulfilment of justice in relationship to God than by the imposition of commandments, laws and temporal sanction related to justice concerned with human beings alone.

How could a truly religious person ever believe he was giving due honour to God if, under cover of religion, he tried to enrich and ennoble himself unduly? He would inevitably sense that he was dishonouring and offending God by depriving him of the worship of human hearts. A person truly desiring to give God what is due to God will never take as his own what belongs to society, to rulers, or to the least amongst mankind. He is extremely careful to give each his own. But those using any pretext whatsoever to be unjust to God show their injustice at the appropriate moment towards their fellow humans. It does happen that divine things are usurped and ruined, and God's kingdom amongst men assaulted, under the pretext of protecting and safeguarding human matters.

488. I believe that we must speak first about the society God wished to form with human beings, his creatures, even on this earth. We call this society 'theocracy' for two reasons; first, because it was the word used by the most famous *jurisconsults*,

all of whom were convinced that divine rights were not to be neglected, but given priority in the whole science of Right [*App.*, no. 1]; second, because our examination of the matter has shown that the society between God and human beings constitutes the solid foundation of every other society: all other societies receive stability and consistency solely from this first, divine society. It must be a cause for amazement that recent treatises on Right, from a rational point of view, have neglected or even obliterated this most important element without realising that they are building civil society in the air, or bringing to light a dead branch of knowledge, an inanimate, headless monster. Such a way of dealing with Right, cut off from religion, has unfortunately legalised the modern impiety that gave it birth. But the separation of religion from Right and from the laws governing Right has gained spurious immortality through its insertion into popular constitutions, where impiety has punished with mockery and incapacity for social life those who doubt its usefulness.

489. But impiety, and all it sets out to achieve, cannot last because it tends to suppress truth and systematic knowledge by eliminating the elements it finds troublesome in them. Human beings have been united by their Creator with truth at the depths of their being, and soon turn back from their mistaken paths in order to seek the sublime element of truth they have discarded, unaware they were throwing away an essential, vital part of themselves. This explains the present universal return, so full of hope, to the religion of Christ which stands at the heart of civil society. A new ardour for Christianity seems to have taken hold of the peoples, rejuvenating religion which appeared to have lost ground in human hearts after nineteen centuries of triumph. Christianity is moving on towards its great destiny: after penetrating individuals, it must penetrate society; after reforming, enlivening and sanctifying every individual thought and longing amongst individuals, it has to do the same at the level of society.

490. It is certain that the influence of the Gospel could never have been brought to bear on human societies if it had not first worked upon individuals; nor could it have taken its place in the science of Right if it had not first been introduced into civil society, where it began its work as soon as rulers entered the

Church. At that time, the Gospel suddenly started to correct
and reform positive legislation. However, its beneficial light did
not penetrate the rational treatment of Right until much later.
This was rendered inevitable in any case by the late development
of rational Right as a science, although the indirect power of the
Gospel, exercised for more than fifteen centuries, finally introduced the first outlines of rational Right in the 16th century and
enabled it to take its place amongst the sciences.

In making *right* immensely superior to *fact*, Christianity destroyed the dominion of fact in the world, and placed right at
the head of nations as their only ruler. By adding to right its own
light and dignity, Christianity gave such importance to right
that it was finally able to appear before the world in its new guise
as an independent, rigorously organised discipline. Christianity
works in secret for the benefit of mankind long before its
capacity becomes apparent. In this way *rational Right*, the tardy
product of religion, appeared as the work of reason; religion, its
progenitor, remained unrecognised in the background, although
it had generated rational Right by perfecting reason and directing its acts. Later, in the works of Grotius, a truly great man, the
Gospel began to be mentioned, but the hour of the world and of
the power of darkness soon caused the good seed to be trampled
underfoot by the enemy when last century's godless publicists
waged what seemed like victorious war against Grotius. Now,
however, it is time to take in hand the work that had to be
abandoned.[1] The difference between *Christian* and all other civil
societies, between the baptised and the unbaptised, is so obvious
that it attracts the attention of politicians of every persuasion. It
is apparent also to non-Christian peoples prepared to admit
their own inferiority, impotence and daily decline, a decline
only delayed by their attempt to imitate the discoveries of
Christianity. Secretly, these peoples live off the crumbs falling
from our table.

491. The immense development unfolded in Christian society
compared with that of other societies is a fact as clear as the
midday sun to those not wishing to shut their eyes to the good
wrought by divine society in the midst of human society. A

---

[1] C. L. Haller has already paid a handsome tribute to H. Grotius in his
Ristorazione della scienza politica.

treatise on social Right cannot abstract from the divine foundation on which the edifice of social Right is raised; the fundamental duties and rights have to be set out first if they are to take
their place as support and complement of the duties and rights
inherent to the edifice. For me, *divine* society is that formed by
God with human beings, and brought to completion by Christianity; this is the society I call *theocratic*. *Divine* and *theocratic*
are both suitable words for describing it.

Anyone not feeling deeply the need for such a treatise, and
preferring to further his own prejudice by leaving the science of
Right cut off from its vital element, should examine the condition of the family and the State deprived of true religion. Before
Christ, how did the family and the State present themselves?
How do they appear now in a Christian light? Such a comparison may not persuade our opponents, but it should certainly
convince them of what we are saying.

492. *Rights* come into existence only if their subject exists; and
they will be effective if someone exists to respect them. These
two conditions can be fulfilled only imperfectly outside Christianity. Outside the sphere of divinely established religion, the
very being of rights is defective, and their effect weakened or
annulled. We will speak briefly about both these conditions,
indispensable for the constitution and realisation of rights, and
about society itself which cannot exist as a complex of rights[2]
unless rights themselves can find a natural basis of subsistence.
If we can prove that rights receive their full being and worth
from Christian society, we shall have proved at the same time
that this society is the basis of all others, and connected with
them as the soul is to the body. It will also be clear that a science
of social Right is bound to be imperfect if it lacks teaching on
the first society which, mother-like, generates, nourishes and
perfects all others.

493. I have maintained that outside Christianity the subject of
rights is either lacking, or certainly weakened and attenuated. I
must now prove this.

If *activity* is the first constitutive of right, it must be granted
that the presence of greater activity denotes the presence of

[2] *ER*, 21–30.

greater rights. It is clear, for example, that a baby has fewer rights than an adult because its activity is almost entirely restricted to that of feeling (feeling, although characterised by passivity, always requires some activity, as we have said).[3] As activity lessens in human beings, therefore, their existence as *subjects* diminishes.

494. The same may be said about *personal activity*, the second constitutive element of right. This depends upon the use of intelligence in human beings; the less it is used, the less a person is a suitable subject of rights. Hence, people suffering from insanity have fewer rights than the sane.

495. It is obvious that as *decent, lawful activity* (the fourth constitutive element of right) diminishes, growth in human wickedness and in unsuitability for a decent, well-ordered life lessens human creatures' aptitude as subjects of right.

496. It is undeniable that Christianity, by introducing divine love into the world, placed therein a *principle of unceasing action* that has immensely increased and perpetuated human activity; the new presence on earth of an indestructible *principle of infinite understanding* cannot be ignored. One obvious result of such a *principle of freedom* is the Christian's sense of his own individuality, which goes hand in hand with the development of his new power of liberty. In contrast, pagan mankind remains subject to fate, and apparently incapable of freely asserting itself. Christianity has certainly improved human behaviour and taught mankind every virtue.[4] This divine religion has restored and increased in human beings the three constitutive elements, activity, understanding and morality, which form the *subject of rights*. Because all human societies are simply a complex or bonding of rights and duties, it is clear that the institution of Christian society must have influenced all other societies, especially domestic and civil society, by revealing new rights within them. Christian society possesses the creative power to extract rights from nothing, as it were, and it strengthens uncertain

---

[3] *ER*, 239. Hence pain cannot lawfully be inflicted on a child; it has the right not to be made to suffer.

[4] On these effects, produced in the Christian world, cf. *Society and its Purpose*, 451–493.

rights at their root by establishing them firmly. It founds and embellishes in mankind the *subject of rights*.

497. But there would be little value in bringing rights into being by saving and developing their subject, if human beings did not respect rights. Even the most factual of rights is valueless if unrespected or bereft of law or power strong enough to protect it.

498. Christianity, by recreating subjects suitable to be invested with human rights, not only raised up these rights from the decadence they shared with fallen human dignity; it also enabled rights to be respected by founding them authoritatively, by sanctioning the moral law that imposes respect for them (the fifth constitutive element of rights), and by recreating persons who would want to give such respect.

499. Christianity did not use force to recreate persons who would respect rights. Respect imposed by force is no longer respect, and its exterior trappings never last.

Christianity compelled human beings to respect rights in the best and most efficacious way by making people want to respect them, as we said. Christianity bettered the human will, and from that moment rights were respected. By providing the world with subjects possessing rights, Christianity also brought into existence those who would freely respect rights. In this way, the realisation of human rights was made possible, and their worth ensured. Domestic and civil society exist in strict dependency upon religious society, which provides for their very essence as well as their perfection. It is impossible to deal with Right in these societies without first speaking of the society in which they are rooted.

500. History proves our argument and shows its validity in every age.

501. Let us examine domestic society first, and consider the individual subjects of right found in it: father, mother, children and servants.[5]

502. The father is strong; the mother, children and servants are weak. All the latter are sacrificed to the former, who is no longer

[5] Properly speaking servants, although living in domestic society, do not form part of it, as we shall see later.

a subject of right but the source of violence and domestic tyranny.

Even if he were a subject of right, no benefit would be gained from dependants who are incapable of feeling or practising the respect that is their duty.

503. What of the rights of woman as wife and mother?

Corruption is always found in non-Christian societies, although it may be present at one of two levels. As soon as society begins to decline, a woman is considered as an instrument for a man's pleasure. At the first level of corruption this instrument is simply degraded in the eyes of her user because the sense of human dignity is not altogether extinguished. At the second level, the degraded instrument is honoured, has great influence in society, and may even be divinised.

504. In the islands of Oceania and the forests of America, the weak sex in families of savages is loaded with the heavy tasks despised by the husband. Often the mother is as subject to her male children as to her husband. She is excluded from their table, forced to depend for food upon the scraps, left without assistance in need, even at the moment of childbirth when brute animals take loving care of their females. Husbands have a general right of life and death over their wives.[6] Without the light of Christian faith, uncivilised man is governed by a constant law that honours force, and despises the weakness he oppresses. Women, considered weak and despicable, are thus condemned to misery twice over.

505. In the East, women are cut off from domestic cares, and abandoned to the eunuchs; they are the victims of well-founded male jealousy, and condemned to perpetual imprisonment. Such a situation indicates the contempt in which they are held, although the general corruption is not so desperate that there is no brake to it. However, this only applies in so far as it benefits dissolute male strength which requires the woman to live for the

---

[6] Caesar thus describes the condition of women amongst the Germanic tribes who, nevertheless, had not reached the level of degradation experienced by other peoples: 'Husbands have the power of life and death over wives and children. When a noble head of family dies, his neighbours meet and normally, if any suspicion arises, decide whether to reduce his wives to the level of slaves' (*De Bello Gallico*, 6: 19).

man's sake. In India, for example, wives have to be burnt on their husbands' funeral pyre.

506. Nevertheless, the harems serving as prisons for women in the East still safeguard the remnants of morality to be found there. There is no doubt that without this kind of despotism, unbridled passion would have reached its lowest level, where empires and popular governments alike are overthrown.[7]

507. This second level of corruption is found in ancient Egypt. Diodorus of Sicily tells of men about to be married promising to remain subject to their wives in all things.[8] Everyone knows what kind of rule women exercised over men in Sparta, and how they ruined the republic.[9] At Rome they shook off the power of domestic rule and censure, and that of public rule and law.[10] The Senate tried in vain to restrain their excesses which finally undermined, corrupted and overthrew the Roman empire.[11]

508. Outside Christianity, therefore, woman is oppressed, or a source of corruption. Their rights are maintained neither by

---

[7] Despotism is one of the principal causes of serraglios and harems (cf. Montesquieu, *De l'Esprit etc.* 7: 9). — Despotic governments are more easily overthrown by immorality because corruption in a despot leads to ruin for his dynasty. Other forms of government fall only as a result of universal corruption. 'The history of China presents us with twenty-two successive dynasties. There were, that is, twenty-two general revolutions, without counting lesser uprisings. — After the reigns of the first three or four rulers, corruption, idleness and softness would overcome their successors, living isolated in their palaces. The spirit, life and family of the dynasty goes into decline as nobles and eunuchs ensure the succession of children. Soon the palace and its useless inhabitants become a danger to the empire. The emperor is then assassinated or eliminated by a usurper who founds a family whose third or fourth successor, in his turn, shuts himself up in his palace' (*ibid.* 7: 7).

[8] Cf. bk. 1. In some parts of India, maternal lineage is held in such honour that daughters succeed to the throne if there are no male heirs. There are also women rulers in Africa.

[9] Cf. Aristotle, *Politics*, 2, 7.

[10] Cf. Montesquieu, 7: 10–14.

[11] Cf. Livy, *Decad* 4, bk. 4, c. 2. A speech of Cato, occasioned by the demand of the tribunes (under pressure from Roman noblewomen) for the abolition of the Oppian law, had this to say, amongst other things, about the women of his time: 'Put a brake on bullying nature and the animal within you. There is no hope that women will act moderately if you do not.'

themselves nor by others. The subject of rights is lacking, rather than the rights themselves.[12]

509. Children in non-Christian families are not what nature requires them to be. Natural laws never retain full, stable force outside Christianity. In the family, all these laws are continually violated with impunity.

510. Parents think they have an absolute right over their children. They arrogantly fix their number; the fewer they are, the deeper the parents' corruption. Superfluous children are prevented or discarded by disorders practised against nature, by abortion, infanticide, selling, exposure. Such means are sometimes forbidden, but ineffectually, by the laws of the State; sometimes they are tolerated, or even permitted; finally, they are commanded, and then justified by the most serious of thinkers![13] How different from the attitude of the apostles sent by the Word Incarnate! They condemned every evil found on the face of the earth because they had received the power to heal it.[14]

[12] When dissoluteness is supreme, women seem incapable of love. This is expressly affirmed by Plutarch in his treatise on love. Cf. also Xenophon in the dialogue entitled *Serine*. Seneca says: 'When woman thinks in solitude, she thinks evil'.

[13] Tacitus describes as extraordinary the Germanic custom of not limiting the number of children (cf. *De Morib. Germ.* §19) — The Roman practice was for the new-born to be placed on the ground at his father's feet; if the father did not pick him up, he was disposed of .— Later, the law allowed only defective and female children to be exposed. Then girls were protected by law, but without practical effect. — According to the law of Lycurgus, babies had to be put at the feet of the elders of clans and tribes who, after examining them physically, would decide whether to have them brought up or exposed (cf. Plutarch in *Lic.*; Müller, *Dor.*, p. 194; C. F. Hermann, *De Causis turbatae apud Lacaedemonios agrorum aequalitatis*, Magdeburg, 1834). — Exposure of children in China is a well-known historical fact. Descriptions of the unnatural methods used by parents to dispose of unwanted children make horrifying reading (cf. *Recherches philosophiques sur les Chinois*, Tom. 1). — It is sufficient to read the outstanding authors of antiquity to be convinced that this plague, which eats away at the essence of domestic society, is incurable without the intervention of Christianity. Plato and Aristotle were prepared to defend it! (cf. *Republic*, 5, *Politics*, 7: 16).

[14] St. Barnabas, a disciple of our Saviour, says in what remains of his letter to the early Christians: 'The foetus is not to be aborted, nor killed after birth. Treat your son and daughter with discipline, and from infancy teach them the fear of the Lord.'

511. Servants living as strangers in the family had even ceased to be human, and consequently could not be the subjects of rights. The rule was: 'A master cannot act unlawfully in his slave's regard'.[15] Cato, the holiest of men according to Seneca,[16] sent flocks of his old, sick slaves to market,[17] and in his treatise on agriculture advised others to avoid wasteful feeding by doing the same.[18] Owners left their slaves to die of on the Tiber Island[19] or used them to feed the fish in their garden ponds.[20] Experiments with poisons were carried out on slaves. They were tortured and punished with instruments that make one shudder.[21] If they coughed or sneezed, they were held guilty of serious crime;[22] if the master of a household was found slain, all the slaves in the place were put to death without trial: 400 perished at the death of Pedianus the second.[23] Female slaves,

[15] And: 'No injury can be done to a slave'. Cf. the Aquilian law, patronised by Caius Aquilius Gallus, *Digest* bk. 9, c. 2, lex 2 and 27; cf. also Cicero, *De Clar. Orat. 34.*

[16] 'Could the gods have found a holier man than Cato to persuade rather than command mankind?'. *Controv. bk. 1, praef.*

[17] Cf. Plutarch, in *Cat.*

[18] Cf. *De Re Rustica.*

[19] Cf. Dio. Cass, bk. 60; Suetonius in *Claud.* 25.

[20] Cf. Pollio.

[21] In one of his plays, Plautus describes some of the furnishing found in Roman houses. It resembles the equipment of a torture-chamber. Modern languages, formed under the influence of Christianity, lack equivalent words to indicate such vile instruments:

> Goads, metal plates, crosses, leg-irons,
> Whips, chains, dungeons, fetters, neck-restraints.
> *As.* 3, 2, 5.

[22] Cf. Seneca, *Letters* 47, 122, where there is a full description of the treatment meted out by masters to their slaves. Cf. also Macrobius *Saturn.* bk. 1, c. 2.

[23] Cf. Tacitus, *Annals*, 14, 44. *Necessity* was used to justify this law. Injustice thus became necessary, made such by preceding injustice! Things had come to such a pass that mankind thought it impossible to continue to exist without injustice. The subject of justice had, in fact, perished. Allow me to quote the words used by Tacitus to justify the injustice of men who knew nothing but injustice. Tacitus' argument may be summed up as follows: further injustice becomes necessary to maintain in force previous injustice which, through loss of correct ideas and language, came to be known as *public utility*. This is what Tacitus actually said: 'Afterwards we have nations in families, with their different rites, when their external sacred signs are practically nothing. At this

The Philosophy of Right

who underwent even greater cruelty at the hands of capricious Roman women,[24] also had to endure disgusting outrages from which their male counterparts were exempt, although the worst depravity of all consisted in the preference shown for young boys and the attempt to change their sex.[25]

512. Every part of *domestic society*, therefore, is defective and cancerous unless upheld by *theocratic society*. Mankind must first be instructed about Right in theocratic society if the rights constituting domestic society are to subsist.

513. Is there a less strict relationship between *civil* and *religious society*? Civil society cut off from religion (which if not true religion is not religion at all) is no longer a complex of actuated rights, but of injustices. In this case, society no longer exists jurally; its place has been taken by destructive, intestine war. Civil society, considered as a union of human beings in accordance with Right, cannot endure without the support of religion.

514. This was the unanimous opinion of the most far-sighted of pagan sages. Cicero says, 'There is no doubt that loyalty and society would vanish, and with them the supreme virtue of justice, if respect for the gods were abolished'.[26]

Plutarch had this to say in a famous passage, 'Travelling around the world, you may well come across cities without walls, literature, kings, houses, comforts, money, schools,

---

stage, you will not produce any result without fear.' — 'But innocent people will perish!' This is the objection. And he answers: 'This is like a flogging in the army. When every tenth person is beaten, even the strong take fright. Every bad example contains SOMETHING WRONG, which is used against individuals for the public good.'

[24] Cf. C. A. Boettinger, *Sabine, ou matinée d'une dame romaine*.

[25] Cf. Suetonius in *Ner.* c. 28. — 'Reports about the revolution at Constantinople, when the Sultan Ahmed was deposed, say that people who pillaged the house of the kehaya did not find one woman there. It is said that things had come to such a point at Algiers that there was not one in most of the harems' (Montesquieu, *De l'Esprit des Lois*, bk. 16: 6). — On the condition of slaves cf. M. de Burigny, *Sur les esclaves romaines*, in Tome 35, *Mémoires de l'Académie Royale des inscriptions et belles lettres*. — cf. Goguet, *Origines des Lois*, etc. Tome 3.

[26] 'If piety towards the gods is done away with, I am afraid that trust and the society of mankind and that most excellent virtue, justice, will all be eliminated with it' (*De Natura Deorum*, bk. 1: 2).

[512–514]

theatres; but you never see a city without temples and gods. Such a city has never been discovered and never will be. It would be easier to build a city in the air than to found a city without gods'.[27] According to Plutarch, civil Right would be built in mid-air unless underpinned by Right proper to religious society. When publicists forgot this, they became responsible for the imperfection still characterising society and the science of social Right.

515. It is greatly to Cicero's honour that he realised the need for respect and reverence if social life were to exist, and indeed if the very possibility of society were to be present amongst mankind. In fact, he went further, openly recognising and declaring that such respect must be sincere, and free from deceit and pretence.[28] But it is impossible to find pure, sincere reverence unassociated with religious truth. Moreover, the foundation of any society can only be true religion, not a vague, general religion or what passes for religion but is in reality impious superstition. Respect and reverence, like every other virtue, is found in truth alone; the 'useful' social deception shamelessly accepted and approved by some publicists as the only religion they recognise is a wicked slur on religion.

516. Right in Christian society, therefore, has to be considered antecedently to Right in civil society, at least by those holding Christianity as the true religion. Christian society is the sole support of both domestic and civil society.

517. Moreover, civil society is made up of families, and outside Christianity the family itself is no longer sound because the rights of its members either lack a subject upon which they depend, or have no power to command respect. Natural relationships in the family are violated or turned on their head. Civil society, formed to maintain the rights of all, cannot be established on this basis. If the families composing civil society are themselves devoid of justice, they certainly cannot practise it towards one another. Civil society no longer exists where chance, in the form of blind passion, rules in the place of Right,

---

[27] *Adversus Colot.*, bk. 2.

[28] 'Piety and the other virtues, along with holiness and religion, can have no place with PRETENCE. But if virtue is eliminated, unease and confusion prevail in life' (*De Nat. Deorum*, bk. 1: 2).

even though the yoke of passion is disguised by jural formulae. Pagan legislation took this stance in its dealings with slaves, gladiators, foreigners, children, women, religious ceremonies, and other matters; public law converted great injustices into civil *rights*.[29] Consequently, these societies were unable to offer human beings a purpose, without which union between humans is no longer society, but an empty imitation of society.[30] Eternal justice, the source of temporal justice, had no sanction in such associations; moral activity, which alone could and would fulfil eternal justice, was lacking to them.[31] These mock societies, degraded by vice, lost their natural form in the degeneration which permitted them to take on one another's forms. In the East, for example, family despotism sometimes became civil despotism; at Rome,[32] civil despotism passed into the family and in the family, born of the republic whose form it borrowed, whole nations were taken captive,[33] as Tacitus says. In a word, it became a monster.

518. Family and civil society, therefore, require as their basis the greater society which God made with human beings, and which Cicero recognised as the source of all laws.[34] It is time to restore to the science of Right its first, fundamental and vital part, which deals with the rights of divine or theocratic society,

[29] Bonald is right when he says: 'It is a sign of ignorance to exaggerate disorders amongst Christians on the one hand, and the virtues of wise pagans on the other, without realising that part of the evil amongst Christians can only be seen in the light of what is essentially virtuous Christian society. Elsewhere, goodness is noticed because other societies are essentially vicious. Christians may indeed do wrong, but their law, which is correct, can and must set things right with its own authority. Amongst idolatrous and non-Christian peoples, life may be decent, but the law is always tainted; and in the last analysis life always conforms to law' (*Essai analytique etc.* p. 102).

[30] As we have shown: cf. *SP*, 235–262, 265–282.

[31] In the *Moral System*, which prefaces the *Philosophy of Right*, it was shown that only the Christian religion: 1. gives sufficient *sanction* to morality; 2. endows mankind with *moral activity*. True and perfect civil society is impossible without these two elements. Cf. *ER*, 214–222.

[32] Cf. *SP*, 337–344, 371–391.

[33] *Nationes in familiis habemus.* Ann. 14: 44. — Sometimes a single Roman citizen had four or five thousand slaves. Cf. Pliny, bk. 33, c. 10 — Juv. *Sat.* 3, 140.

[34] *De Legibus*, 1.

and enable this science to be integrated and attain the perfection proper to its own form.

519. However, learned people, accustomed to rigorous, scientific method, may feel it out of place to want to introduce revealed religion (and Christianity at that!) in a treatise on rational Right. Let us reply to this scientific concern before going further, in order to prevent methods of procedure from prejudicing the essential core of the question, in which alone we are truly interested.

520. First, our aim in these volumes is to study the *philosophy of Right*, as the title indicates, rather than *rational Right*. Philosophy of Right means the philosophy of every right, and this is sufficient to free us from the shackles of a method concerned only with an abstract Right of reason.

521. However, we should point out that rational Right itself cannot abstract completely from certain facts concerning mankind.

522. If a philosopher studying rational Right wished to abstract from all facts, whether natural or dependent on our will, he would lack a component part of his science, and be unable to construct any portion of it.

The sole acceptance of human nature as a bare possibility would not provide a way of initiating his study. Of itself, human nature does not include the fact of *coexistence* amongst human beings; it requires only the possibility of an individual who as such cannot possess rights in his own regard.[35]

Hence the study of Right could not begin without supposing two ideal facts, that is, the possibility of human beings, and the possible co-existence of several human individuals. The mind can only conceive of Right after having perceived these two ideal facts or data because, as we have said, the concept of right lies in a relationship between a plurality of intelligent beings.

523. It is true that the concept of right would be present, granted only the two facts of human nature and co-existence, but our systematic knowledge could make no progress. Only the first page of rational Right would be written, and the book we have produced on the *essence of right* would be sufficient to

[35] Cf. *ER*, 299.

complete the treatise. *Derived Right* would be non-existent; there would be no possibility of dealing either with right as principle or with the way in which rights are derived

524. If special human rights are to be studied, it is necessary to posit in the treatise itself the *titles* from which they spring. These titles are ideal or possible facts, as we have said, to which the notion of right, that is, the principle of the science of Right, is applied. Special rights have their source in such titles in so far as the titles themselves take their place as objects of jural reason.

525. If rational Right is extended, as it must be, to the derivation and determination of special rights, it cannot prescind from certain ideal facts pertaining both to the essence and the accidental states of human nature

It now remains to be seen what facts have to be excluded from this science if it is not to be confused with similar or coterminous sciences. Can religious facts be admitted, and if so, which of them? If the principle of Right is applied to religious facts, what special rights and jural consequences result?

526. In the first place, *rational Right* has to exclude the facts proper to *positive Right*.

527. Positive Right has certain facts in common with rational Right, and certain facts proper to itself.

528. Let us take any problem concerned with Right. For example, after the three years of non-payment of interest, is there a jural obligation of payment, or does the obligation cease through prescription? The problem can be solved according to *rational Right*, and according to *positive Right*. We have a fact common to both branches of Right. It is of little importance whether the fact is ideal and presumed, or real. Common facts, facts presumed as possible, are present in *rational Right* and *positive Right* as the concern of both kinds of legislation.

529. Besides these facts, there are others *proper* to positive Right. They are those *positive laws* which resolve cases of Right. Positive laws, that is, laws dependent upon arbitrary enactment, are the facts proper to positive Right.

530. We can conclude, therefore: the facts to be excluded from treatises on derived rational Right are the positive facts of the legislator, the arbitrary decisions of the legislator; in a word, the laws established by the will of the legislator.

531. In the second place, rational Right must exclude, generally

speaking, the facts proper to *applied Right*. These are real facts, or more exactly the reality of these facts. Rational Right is not interested in knowing whether the facts or cases it considers really exist or not. It simply treats them *as possible*. *Positive Right* does the same. *Laws* are not made for real, particular cases, which are the object of the findings of the judge, who has to apply the law. If laws were merely decisions made in real, particular cases, there would be no need of judges; legislation and legislators would disappear. Only decisions would remain, without positive laws or judge.[36]

532. Nevertheless, an important exception has to be made to this general truth.

It depends upon the distinction between real *contingent* facts, and real *necessary* facts.

Rational Right has to prescind from the reality of contingent facts, but is this the case with the reality of necessary facts? This question can be answered only by first seeing whether rational Right is *able* to prescind from the reality of necessary facts. And our reply is clear if we reflect that *necessary fact* indicates a fact which, if thought as *possible*, must also be judged to be *really existent*. In a necessary fact there can be no separation between its *possibility* and its *subsistence*; either the fact has to be prescinded from totally, or has to be considered as subsistent.

Having made this qualification, we can now see that the scope of *derived rational Right* is to indicate, according to the dictate of reason, all the *rights* of intelligent beings in every case and circumstance.

Rational Right prescinds from the reality of contingent cases because decisions about them would be endless, like the cases themselves. Moreover, contingent reality is not necessary for the end in view. When rights have been established according to ideal facts, real rights are immediately discovered by the application of the ideal to the real cases. Ideal cases indeed contain all that can be known about the real cases corresponding to them.

The possibility of this application arises from the separation, present in contingent beings, between the ideal, possible case

---

[36] Cf. *ER*, 49–53.

and the real case. The latter, which is multiple, is seen in and through the former, which is unique.

But what must be said if the *ideal case* and the *real case* are so joined that they cannot be distinguished without their being annihilated? It is obvious that rational Right could not attain its purpose of deriving and determining *all rights possible* to intelligent nature without accepting this strange mode of facts that are necessarily real, but have no ideal separate from themselves to which they can be referred, and through which they can be known.

We have to ask ourselves, therefore, which facts are essentially real and not solely ideal. In formulating this question we are also asking about facts that give rise to real rights only, without reference to ideal rights. Such real rights are all those founded on the existence of the supreme Being whose reality is so necessary that a merely possible and non-subsistent God cannot be thought of. A possible God would be no God. *Absolute being*, and consequently being in all its forms, including its reality, is essential to God.[37]

Granted, therefore, that *derived rational Right* has as its aim the determination of all rights, it is evident: 1. that it cannot consider contingent facts except in their *ideality*; 2. nor necessary facts except in their *reality*.

533. Necessary facts, as we said, are those founded in necessary being. We shall call them, therefore, *humanitarian-religious* facts. There is no species corresponding to these facts, but simply the individual facts in the very nature of things. They have to be taken for what they are, and as they are, or as they have happened.

534. We can conclude that scientific method does not repudiate such facts. Scientific method has to harmonise and measure up to the end a determined science wishes to attain; a method rendering impossible the attainment of the proposed aim of a

[37] Cf. *Certainty*, 1044–1377. Malebranche had some notion of this truth, without being able to express it exactly. He wrote: 'Nothing finite can represent the infinite, and the idea of God is necessarily God himself.' These words: 1. suppose falsely that the idea is a *representation*, which it is not; and 2. state that 'the idea of God is God', instead of saying that no *positive idea* of God is possible, but only a *perception of God*.

science cannot be wholesome. Derived rational Right sets out to expound 'every species of human rights', including those which accrue to human beings from divine, necessarily real facts. The Right of theocratic society has every reason, therefore, to form part of rational Right. Without it, rational Right would inevitably be deficient, weak, and mistaken in its conclusions.

These arguments put to rest scientific unease about method. We can now begin our study of the first part of *Right in particular societies*, hoping that our description of the relationships and bonds uniting human beings with the supreme Being, will clarify, demonstrate and authoritatively establish the relationships and bonds between human beings themselves.

DISTRIBUTION OF THE SUBJECT-MATTER

535. In all societies, including theocratic society we must distinguish the three elements indicated in our treatise on universal rights (cf. 145–153): the *seigniorial*, the *governmental* and the *communal*.

These three elements, already outlined by us, will provide the subject-matter and divisions in the present book in which we shall deal in order with the seigniorial, the governmental and the communal rights of theocratic society.

SECTION ONE

THE RIGHT OF SEIGNIORY IN
THEOCRATIC SOCIETY

CHAPTER 1
The supreme being is the only Lord

536. This truth is perfectly well-known to human common sense. There is nothing more obvious than the title given by holy Scripture to the supreme Being, who is the 'ONE LORD'.[38]

537. The evident truth of these words is equalled by the depth of their meaning; everyone can accept them, yet few can fully penetrate them. The uniqueness of dominion is equal to the uniqueness of being. The profoundly true meaning of the ancients' wise saying, 'God alone is, other things are not,'[39] is matched by the equally profound statement, 'God is the only Lord, and apart from him there is no lord'. It is surely evident that dominion cannot be exercised by what is not.

CHAPTER 2
The fullness and absoluteness of divine seigniory

538. There is no seigniory except God's, which is essential and fully absolute.

539. Natural reason, as well as revelation, affirms without

---

[38] Eph 4: 5.

[39] St. Augustine says: 'And I looked at the things below you, and I saw that they neither are nor are not in every sense. They are because they are through you; they are not because they are not what you are. That truly is which remains unchangeably' (*Conf.*, 7: 9).

doubt this fullness of dominion, expressed very succinctly by St. Paul, 'In him we live and move and have our being'.[40] That is, we owe our existence to him as to the one who has made us pass from non-being to being. We also owe him our existence at every moment, and everything that we have along with existence. All things subsist by power of that divine act which continually makes them subsist as they are at every instant and as they operate.

CHAPTER 3

There is only one servitude

540. It follows directly that, as there is only one Lord, so there is only one servitude.

541. This principle is also the basis of the government exercised by God over his creatures. He wanted it written at the beginning of the positive legislation he gave to his people, 'You shall worship the Lord, your God, and HIM ONLY SHALL YOU SERVE'[41] These words clearly command two things: the *worship* of God, and care to safeguard one's *freedom* from all service that is not divine.

Worship is the acknowledgement of the unique, absolute dominion of the supreme Being, by which the creature willingly submits himself to God. This full, voluntary submission to the supreme Being involves the necessity of not serving anything else because any other service would diminish that due to God. Every other service completely ceases to be such when compared with that of God.

[40] Acts 17: 28.
[41] Deut 6: 13; 10: 20.

CHAPTER 4

The servitude due to God is full and absolute

542. Consequently, the servitude owed to God is full and absolute.

543. Does this absolute servitude imply a right in God over our very personality in such a way that he can use it as a pure means?

544. The human person is an end because of the divine element which informs it.[42] This element, which in God is God, cannot be employed as a simple means even by God himself who, being essentially end, cannot use himself as means. Hence Scripture says that God made himself the end of all things, and could not do otherwise.[43]

545. He is end, therefore, in so far as he communicates himself to humankind, either through the light of reason or through gifts superior to nature. This teaching, which ennobles human creatures, is echoed in divine Scripture when it says that God, in his absolute, all-powerful dominion, treats mankind 'with great reverence'.[44]

CHAPTER 5

The nature of divine seigniory

546. In order to know the fullness of *divine rights* relative to human creatures, it is necessary to consider the unique nature of

---

[42] *Principles of Ethics*, 101–105.

[43] 'The Lord has made all things for himself' (Prov 16: 4 [Douai]).

[44] 'You are master of power, you judge with tranquillity, and with GREAT REVERENCE dispose of us' (Wis 12: 18). The words, 'you judge with tranquillity', are also worthy of attention. God Almighty uses his power with 'calm judgement', which conforms to reason and lacks passion. He never sacrifices what is reasonable to his power; what is reasonable is always the end of his activity.

[542–546]

divine seigniory over mankind. Such seigniory has to be preserved intact from all human laws, and safeguarded. Human laws, if they are to be just, must in fact be founded on divine seigniory.

547. Divine seigniory is both *de facto* and *de iure* seigniory. It will help if we say a word about both, because seigniory by right is very closely connected with seigniory in fact.

Article 1.
Divine *de facto* dominion over mankind

548. God, who is essential, complete and absolute being, must have in himself the three forms of being, that is, *ideality*, *reality* and *morality*.

549. Through these forms of being, he exercises absolute, *de facto* dominion in three modes over mankind.

550. God, so far as he has the form of ideality, that is, in so far as he is as ideal being, communicates to human beings the knowledge of *good* as such.

551. The knowledge of *what is good as such* is an element in the formation of the human will, because the will itself is simply an inclination towards good without determination or specification. Such an inclination is the will in first act, through which the will as potency is in being.

Human beings can choose between one good and another, but they can never choose that which the *practical reason* does not judge as good. They are inclined, therefore, towards good as such by an unavoidable necessity of nature. Thus, absolute, *de facto* dominion is exercised by God over his creatures through the communication of himself to them as *ideal being*.[45]

552. God, in so far as he has the form of reality, that is, in so far as he is real being without qualification, exercises absolute,

---

[45] Relative to the intellect, *ideal being* is called 'exemplary truth' when beheld in relationship to things; the intellect is completely subject to ideal being as exemplary truth. Relative to the will, *being* as intuited in the idea is called 'good as such', and has full command and direction of the human will. I have preferred to consider being as *what is good* because as such it dominates the *personal activity* of human beings.

de facto dominion over mankind through *creation* and *conservation*, and through *providence* by which he disposes and orders all that occurs. Through creation, he makes creatures subsist; conserving them, he gives them the reality of being at every successive moment of time, so that if they were not sustained by his creating power they would *ipso facto* cease; finally, through his providence, he harmonises the different measures of being and the different forces given to his creatures so that all may move together towards the realisation of the great design he has conceived from eternity.

553. The Creator's great design is that creatures, through the quantity of action he bestows on them, may come to know and glorify him in the best way possible, thus realising in themselves the greatest quantity of holiness and happiness which result from the practical knowledge they have of God and the consequent glory they render him. We can rightly affirm, therefore, that the glory of God is the unfailing end of the universe. Human free will is in service to this end with the same infallibility as that of necessary agents in nature; wicked persons themselves are necessary means for reaching it. Divine Scripture says that the will of God will be done in its entirety, and that his design, conceived from eternity and announced at the beginning will finally attain completion from the course of all events. His dominion, therefore, is absolute; nothing can frustrate it.[46]

554. Finally, in so far as the form of *morality* is in God, he has *de facto* dominion for realising his justice by bestowing bliss on the just, and merited unhappiness on the unjust. This dominion also is absolute, and cannot be resisted in any way by any being. Good persons are destined for peace and joy; those who dwell in heaven cannot but love God, who reigns in them without impediment as the power bringing them bliss. Remorse and torment are reserved for evil-doers; those condemned to hell cannot but fear God without limit, experiencing him as the power that punishes with great equity. This kind of *de facto*

[46] 'I am God, and there is none like me,
  declaring the end from the beginning
    and from ancient times things not yet done,
  saying, "My counsel shall stand,
    and I will accomplish my purpose"' (Is 46: 9–10).

dominion also has no conceivable limits, nor opposition of any sort.

555. The *de facto dominion* exercised by the supreme Being over mankind is therefore threefold, and results in a threefold necessity: the moral necessity of following *good*; the necessity of accomplishing the eternal, divine design; the necessity of the triumph of justice through inexorable, ineffable rewards, and through inevitable, ineffable punishments.

Article 2.
Divine *de iure* dominion over mankind

556. God's *right of dominion* over mankind is also threefold because the three modes of being considered in God constitute three original titles of absolute and essential right.

§1. *God is truth:*
the first title to the right of supreme dominion

557. The first of these titles is that of truth: God is subsistent truth.

558. We have shown that the principle of morality consists in truth; morally speaking truth is the primal, originating force of obligation for mankind.[47]

Every morally obliging authority and force is founded essentially in the light of truth.

Hence God, as subsistent *truth*, is not *any title* of dominion, but a *supreme title* from which all other *titles* receive their obligating force. God, as such, has by his essence the right of supreme dominion over intelligent creatures; this dominion synthesises and simplifies in itself every other juridical dominion.

---

[47] Cf. *ER*, 103–107.

§2. God is the principle of being for creatures: the second title to the right of supreme dominion

559. The second title is that of principle of being: God is the cause of creatures; he is their Creator.

560. Every creature, therefore, and every entity found in creatures, is the *absolute property* of God, posited by God at every moment.

561. Creatures must conform to the will of the Creator. Otherwise, they would be attempting to violate the divine right of ownership by trying to impede the owner from using what is his in the way he wishes.

562. Because nothing is so closely united with and dependent upon human beings as their own union and dependence upon the act with which God posits them, God's ownership is more immediate and universal than any other.

§3. God is holiness and bliss: the third title to the right of supreme dominion

563. The third title is that of absolute good: God is essential holiness and bliss.

564. It follows from this title that human beings do not attain the final good of holiness and eternal happiness unless they draw them from God.

565. It is necessary for human beings to acknowledge God as the supreme fount of their perfection. If they are not informed by God, essential holiness and bliss, they cannot themselves possess, nor find elsewhere, the full attainment of that which constitutes their end.

566. Acknowledging one's end in God involves acknowledging absolute dependence upon God. This dependence is such that man loses himself if he does not receive from God what saves and perfects him.

567. Hence this final title springs from the moral necessity incumbent upon persons of receiving perfection.[48]

[48] Cf. *ER*, 215–222.

§4. *In God the three supreme categorical formulae of morality
become three separate titles of supreme dominion*

568. What has been outlined here shows that the three titles of
divine dominion over mankind respond to the three categorical
forms of morality studied in *Conscience*.[49]

Chapter 6

How divine dominion possesses
the nature of right

569. It may be objected that it is difficult to see how the third
of the five constitutive elements of right is present in God. We
have defined this element as, 'a good inherent in the activity
forming the subject of right'.[50] God does not in fact receive from
creatures any good that can make him more blissful. His dominion over them, therefore, has no value for him, it would seem,
and hence lacks the *good* which is an essential element of right.
The notion of right, therefore, would not seem to be present in
God.

570. It is true that God's bliss, which is essential to him, can
neither increase nor decrease. The divine essence is itself divine
bliss. At the same time we have to note that the free act with
which God from eternity has created things in time, ruling and
governing them, is not in him really different from his substance. Granted his free will in creating the universe, dominion
over it belongs to his divine substance. Considered like this,
dominion is not only a good for God, but an infinite good; it is
his very own bliss because it is not really distinct from his
substance. The third constitutive element of right, that is, good
as inherent in activity, is not lacking from divine right, therefore,

---

[49] 162–175, 198 — The most universal principle of morality is an abstract
formula, implying the three categorical forms. It does not, therefore, provide
a fourth title of right.

[50] Cf. *ER*, 252–255.

but is fully present in God, where it is infinite, supreme and so complete that rights in other beings cannot compare with it.

571. It may still be objected that there is no possibility of jural damage to this right because no one can inflict harm or pain on God. We answer that damage to right does not consist only in harming or paining the subject of right; it is also present when this is attempted.[51]

572. Two important truths follow from this: 1, a person refusing to acknowledge divine dominion, or attempting to withdraw from it, attempts to destroy the divine essence; 2, such an act is not only *unjust* to the highest degree, but in addition ignorant and *foolish*.

CHAPTER 7

Three marks of divine seigniory over human beings

What has been said indicates three sublime marks of divine seigniory over human beings: it is *reasonable, natural* and highly *beneficial*, although the beneficiary is not the lord, but his servants.

Article 1.
Divine seigniory is reasonable

573. The first of the three titles we have indicated in divine seigniory gives rise to its *reasonableness*.

574. This title consists in the authority inherent in *ideal being*, the form of every intellect. It is obvious that servitude to God, as the first and supreme reason, is not only reasonable, but is *reasonableness* itself. Acting reasonably, and obeying or serving ideal being, is one and the same thing.

---

[51] Cf. *ER*, 360.

Article 2.
Divine seigniory is natural

575. The second title on which divine seigniory is founded, that is, God as the principle of every contingent being, gives rise to the *naturalness* of divine seigniory.

576. It is a universal, ontological law that everything aspires and tends to unite itself with its principle, provided we understand 'principle' as the fount of a thing's being and of everything that belongs to its being. This law, as we have already noted, is marvellously unfolded in human activity. In fact, human beings are so constituted that every being is a good for them, and a greater good if greater being.[52] But an entity, to be such for human beings, must be known by them. To be good for them, knowledge of the entity must be their own work, that is, human beings must want to know the entity as good. To know it as good is to esteem it; this constitutes what we call *practical knowledge*. If, however, human beings are not active relative to knowledge but merely passive, their knowledge is incomplete; it remains in the form we have called *theoretical knowledge*, which is ineffective because it does not put human beings in *real* communication with known entities. Only when humans contribute to knowledge their own spontaneous activity by which they unite themselves with what has been understood, does a being as known become for them the principle of all their special activity, including their exterior activity.[53] In this case, they act intelligently as a result of their will which, at its origin, is simply the faculty enabling them to understand forcefully and feelingly relative to the object understood.[54] All beings are destined to be

---

[52] Cf. *PE*, 21–42.

[53] Cf. *ER*, 108–112.

[54] Hegel was aware of this truth, but he exaggerated it. When he says: *Der Wille ist eine besondere Weise des Denkens*, he expresses the truth; when he adds that the will is *das Denken als sich übersetzend ins Dasein*, he still states the truth, but his metaphorical way of speaking inclines him to overstep himself if *übersetzend* (passing) is not interpreted properly. At this point, however, he further explains his thought, adding: *als Trieb sich Dasein zu geben* (*Grundlinien der Philosophie des Rechts, oder Naturrecht und Staatswissenschaft im Grundrisse*. Berlin, 1833. *Einleitung*). This produces the ambiguity that destroys his system in which, having reduced will to thought,

good for humans in this way; greater beings are greater good; and the greatest being of all is the maximum good. God, the being of beings, is rightly called by St. Augustine 'the good of every good' (*bonum omnis boni*). If something is good for human beings, it must somehow perfect and complete their nature; but the ultimate completion and sublimation of human nature is the possession of God.

577. It is clear, therefore, that human nature tends to God because it must tend towards its highest good as a result of tending towards good as such.

578. Human servitude to God consists in such a tendency of human nature, seconded and determined by will. This servitude, therefore, is entirely in harmony with human nature. Divine seigniory, on its part, is wholly *natural* to human nature.

Article 3.
Divine seigniory benefits the servants, not the lord

579. The third mark of divine seigniory is unlimited *disinterestedness* and beneficence.

580. As we have said, God would not be less God, nor less perfect and blissful, if he had not wished to create the world. In creating it, he acquired nothing that he did not have previously, and is now as he was from eternity. His creative act has not changed him.

581. The world, and the reverence the supreme Being receives from the world's inhabitants, produces no benefit for God. All the benefit is for human beings alone whose highest good lies

he also wants to assimilate the objects of thought to thought itself, converting them into his hold-all idea which includes everything. It is true that the will tends to bestow on itself an ever greater degree of being and perfection; it is also true that it tends to make beings its own; but it does not tend to make them ITSELF. Hegel, despite his acuteness, did not see that it is impossible to reduce subject and object to a single principle; he did not see that they are two primitive, original forms of being which cannot be confused, although they necessarily exist together, complementing and perfecting one another. It is, in fact, their unremitting, absolute distinction which lies at the basis of their relationship.

[577–581]

precisely in the servitude they render him to serve him is to reign.

582. We need to think of the matter in this way. Granted the act with which the Creator has freely willed to give subsistence to contingent beings, this act, containing creation, conservation, providence, judgment, reward, and so on, is undivided from the act with which he is. But the act with which God is, the act of divine essence, has suffered no change, nor has it become greater or fuller related to exterior works. Consequently, God's bliss has not increased. On the contrary, although the creatures' act in offering him worship adds nothing to him, it does bring perfection to them, just as an act opposed to the worship of the supreme Being does great damage to them by depriving them of their moral perfection and integrity.[55]

583. Such an argument cannot be understood completely unless a careful distinction is made between subjective and objective good. Only by grasping this distinction can we see how moral evil, committed by creatures when they dishonour God, is 'an objective evil done by a subject'. The subject neither harms nor can harm the object, essentially immune from all damage, but does great harm to himself.

584. It follows that the servitude due to God implies no obligation whatever to give something to God in a true sense, as though he as subject could receive something from us. But it does imply an obligation to reverence him as object, not because this object, considered as subject, can be benefited, but simply because he as object is unchangeable, remaining what he is. When we adapt ourselves to the exigency of the object, which in our case is an exigency of absolute subjection, we simply do what is good in itself. The natural effect of this good is to enoble and enlighten us.

585. We can now see more clearly how divine seigniory is

---

[55] St. Augustine's wonderful statement about God: 'For you had no need of me, nor am I some kind of good that you need, my Lord and my God. I am not here to help you, as though you would grow tired without me, nor is your power less if it lacks my respect. I do not cultivate you as though you were land that would remain desolate without my labour. I serve you and I cultivate you THAT I MAY BENEFIT FROM YOU. YOU HAVE MADE ME THAT I MAY BE FOR YOU, O MY GOOD. (*Confessions*, bk. 13, c. 1, cf. also c. 4).

essentially different from every other. Every other seigniory exists for the lord's benefit, not for that of the servant; every other seigniory has the master as its end as worthy of respect and as beneficiary. Divine seigniory is quite different: the master is indeed the end of the servant, but it is the servant alone who benefits, and to the greatest extent, from such a state. Because the servant alone benefits by his servitude, his service does not diminish his standing as end. Thus we come to understand more profoundly the words of Scripture we quoted above, 'He disposes of men WITH GREAT REVERENCE'.

CHAPTER 8

Divine seigniory is inalienable

586. Dominion is proper to the supreme Being because of his divine essence. It is therefore as inalienable as the divine essence itself.

CHAPTER 9

Servitude before God demands three acts: morality, worship and obedience

587. Three acts of human servitude respond to the three titles of divine seigniory.

588. The necessity of conforming all our activities to the rational order, wherein lies *morality*, responds to God's title as truth, as ideal being.

589. The necessity of acknowledging God as principle of every being, of adoring him and sacrificing to him,[56] of drawing close to him in every way in order to attract him, as it were, to

---

[56] Sacrifice is the act by which creatures annihilate themselves, as it were, in order to show effectively their acknowledgement of the Creator's infinite seigniory.

us, wherein lies *worship*, responds to the God's title as real Being.

590. The necessity of harmonising every human wish with the divine will, however it may be known, responds to the God's title as holiness, as moral being, wherein consists positive *obedience* which, if perfect, not only fulfils the express commands, but also the counsels of the supremely good Lord.

591. These three acts of servitude are categorically distinct, although each one involves and supposes the others.

592. In fact, *morality* prescribes worship and the obedience to be given to God; *worship* is not perfect without morality and obedience; *obedience* cannot be conceived in an immoral person who does not offer worship to God. None of these acts can stand without the others.

593. Nevertheless, it is helpful to distinguish them mentally from one another. First, because the titles in which they are founded are distinct. Second, because the obligations expressly contained in each of these acts is only potentially or virtually present in the others. For example, the act of 'living according to reason' is contained expressly in morality, which, however, refers only implicitly and virtually to worship and obedience. In worship, the obligation of acknowledging the seigniory of the supreme Being in our interior and exterior actions is actual and expressed, but its conformity with reason is present only implicitly. In obedience, the immediate purpose is our submission to the will of the supreme Being; the obligation of worship and of morality has to be argued from this.

594. Very often these three things have been separated, with great harm to man's duty of submission to God. Mistakes have been made in three ways.

595. *Morality* has been opposed to worship and obedience. It has been maintained that morality alone includes all divine worship, and all obedience to the being who is essentially reason. God as reality and holiness has been ignored.

596. *Worship* has been opposed to morality and obedience. It has been maintained that man's duty to God is fulfilled when worship has been satisfied (and in this case, worship is commonly understood as chiefly composed of exterior ceremonies). It has been forgotten that God is not only the principle of being, but also absolute reason and holy will.

[590–596]

597. Finally, *obedience* has been opposed to morality and worship. It has been maintained that man has no further obligation towards his Creator when he has fulfilled his *positive*, external commands, the letter of the law, not the spirit. God, as supreme reason and holy will to which man owes interior submission of will and heart, has been ignored.

598. Each of these errors resulted from the formation of imperfect concepts of morality, worship and obedience to God, because the implicit content of the concept was separated from their immediate content. Conclusions to be argued from what was implicit were ignored.

599. Each of these three summary duties constituting servitude due from creatures to the Creator possesses an unchangeable part, springing from it directly, and a part more or less developed depending upon the progress made by mankind.

600. The immediate, unchangeable part of *morality* is the imperative, 'Follow the light of reason'. Its deduced and developed part are the particular imperatives formed by varying applications of the light of moral reason to changing and evolving circumstances.

601. The immediate, unchangeable part of *worship* is the imperative, 'Acknowledge with your whole self the supreme dominion of the supreme Being'. Its deduced, developed part are the various acts of worship contained implicitly in this practical acknowledgement. These acts can vary and increase according to changeable circumstances, and independently of our will.

602. The immediate, unchangeable part of *obedience* is the imperative, 'Obey the divine will'. Its deduced, developed part is made up of the various acts of obedience rendered necessary by better rational interpretation, more in harmony with the divine will, or by God's positive manifestation of his will in various matters.

CHAPTER 10

Three acts of dominion exercised by God
towards his creatures

603. Acts of *dominion* have to be distinguished from acts of mere *power*.

604. All God's acts form part of his *power*, but acts of *dominion*, as I call them, refer immediately to the servitude due to him from human creatures.

605. The servitude given to God by human beings is in part necessary, and in part free. Hence the distinction between *de facto* and *de jure* dominion.[57] We see that God forms his intelligent creatures to acknowledge him as supreme Lord either by means of their necessitated will (for example, in their tendency towards good in general) or in spite of their will (the damned, for example, have to believe in God's divine power notwithstanding their recalcitrance). In forming his creatures like this, God certainly exercises an act of just dominion over them.

606. However, we do not wish to consider the power of God, but those acts of dominion which God exercises simply by right. In this case he uses his right of seigniory, but at the same time leaves human beings free to act or not in accordance with their servitude. These divine acts can be reduced to three kinds:

1. The rational law, and God's positive commands (the divine-positive law).

2. External circumstances, directed by his Providence to obtaining the greatest servitude from his intelligent creatures. These circumstances manifest his will as soon as the law is applied to them.

3. The communication of himself, as real being, to human beings. Through this communication he establishes his reign in souls (this is the order of grace and of glory).[58]

[57] Cf. 546–648.

[58] The dominion of grace is sublimely expressed by St. Augustine when, addressing God, he says of the Holy Spirit: 'Here we shall rejoice in you, our resting place. Love lifts us to this point, and your good Spirit raises our

607. It is easy to see that these three kinds of acts of seigniory respond to the three supreme modes in which the human mind thinks being.

CHAPTER 11

The ministers of God's dominion over human beings

608. God exercised his dominion over human beings both immediately, and by means of the services of ministers from amongst his intelligent creatures.

609. Scripture tells us that he sometimes used angels, and sometimes holy people, to represent him for this purpose.

610. Through his ministers he communicated his positive law to human beings, and worked many wonders to arouse the servitude owed by humans and ardently desired by him.

CHAPTER 12

The dominion of Christ

611. The greatest, sublimest of these ministers is Christ.

612. But Christ is not only God's minister. It is necessary, therefore, to examine the other properties and attributes of Christ relative to divine seigniory.

613. They are six: he is 1. *supreme Lord* (God); 2. *servant of*

lowliness from the gates of death. In your will is our peace. Our body tends under its weight to its own place, either below or whither it truly belongs. Fire reaches up, stone bears down; they are under the influence of their different weights, they seek their proper place. Oil spread on water remains on the surface; water sinks when spread on oil. They are under the influence of their own weights, they seek their proper place. If they are not ordered as they should be, they are not at rest; if ordered, they rest. My weight is my love; it bears me wherever I am borne. We are set aflame by your gift, and immediately we are borne on high. Inflamed, we move and ascend the inclines of our heart, singing the canticle of the ascents' (*Confessions*, bk. 13, c. 11).

God; 3. *the human being who is Lord over other human beings;* 4. *God's minister for the salvation of the world;* 5. *judge of the world;* and 6. *head of the Church.* We shall say a few words about each of these properties.

Article 1.
Christ is of himself supreme Lord

614. Christ is God as well as man. As God, he has divine, inalienable dominion.

615. One of the divine prerogatives is to be light, a ray of which makes human beings naturally intelligent.

Because this light enables moral good and evil to be discerned, it is also law. All Christians do in fact conceive of Christ as light and law; for them, such undoubted teaching is understood as the foundation of their faith. An obvious proof that Christians conceive of Christ as objective reason itself (which enabled Christ to say, 'I AM THE WAY') can be seen in their attitude towards morality. All Christians acknowledge that Christ reproves and condemns whatever is immoral; they also recognise every moral virtue as conforming to Christ. Christians do not look in the Gospel for any express, particular condemnation of wickedness, or praise of virtue. Their judgement is as it were *a priori*, and is deduced immediately from the concept they have of Christ which tacitly supposes the belief that 'to oppose moral reason' is the same as opposing Christ in whom this reason subsists.

For St. Paul, this explains the great difference between the Hebrew law and the Gospel. The former contained particular moral formulae, expressed in words, but the light itself, moral reason, remained hidden. The Gospel, however, gives us the light in its supernatural fullness, because it gives us Christ. 'And even if our Gospel is veiled,[59] it is veiled only to those who are

---

[59] The Hebrews covered the book of the law with a veil in a ceremony recalling Moses' veiling of his face, which shone as he spoke to the people. St. Paul refers to this symbol as an indication that the Hebrews were not given light, the truth itself, but only signs foreshadowing it.

perishing. In their case the god of this world has blinded the minds of the unbelievers, to keep them from seeing the light of the Gospel of the glory of Christ, who is the LIKENESS OF GOD. For what we preach is not ourselves, but JESUS Christ as Lord,[60] with ourselves as your servants for JESUS' sake. For it is the God who said, "Let light shine out of darkness", who has shone in our hearts to give the light of the knowledge of the glory of God in THE FACE OF JESUS'.[61] This is not the bodily face of Christ, but the concept, the perception, we have of him. In this concept and perception we find 'the knowledge of the glory of God', perfect moral teaching, the doctrine of holiness, which reaches its fullness in the knowledge of God.

616. Plato, and many others, thought it a prerogative of the divinity to be 'reason itself'; wise men in the East had come to the same conclusion long before. This explains why they affirmed regal dignity to be a power delegated by God; they intended to subject it to moral reason. A modern author has this to say in explaining the teaching of Chinese philosophers, 'Chinese political and moral authors recognised that extreme absolute power in the heads of government was never more than a power delegated by Heaven, that is, by SUPREME ABSOLUTE REASON . . . This absolute power is subject to moral limits that cannot be gainsaid. If the mandate is abused by infraction of these moral laws, the people are freed from all respect and obedience towards such power (according to Tchou-hi, a celebrated Chinese philosopher of the 12th century, in his Commentary on the first of the four classical books of China, which was used in all the schools and colleges of the Empire)'. Another legitimate power takes the place of that which has been so completely overthrown.[62]

[60] The phrase 'to preach Christ' had not been used about a human being or human teacher before Christ came into the world. One does not preach man, but doctrine, truth. But the phrase is very appropriate when applied to the master who is truth.

[61] 2 Cor 4: 3–6.

[62] G. Pauthier, *Les Livres Sacrés de l'Orient*, Paris, 1840, Introduction.

Article 2.
Christ is also servant of God

617. As man, Christ is servant of God.

618. Christ as man is not only a servant of God, like all other creatures; he is the most sublime of God's servants. In Scripture we read that God formed this perfect servant from his mother's womb.[63]

619. Christ is not only the sublimest servant. He is the only faithful servant; all other humans *have fallen away*.[64] All alike are disqualified for the service of God, the great end of creation.

620. Only in Christ has God obtained full servitude from a creature, the end for which he created the universe.

621. He attained servitude superabundantly in Christ because Christ, as man, gave God all the service of which elevated human nature is capable. But this was not the only reason. Christ is also God; his activity is *theandric*, and what he does has infinite value; his activities constitute infinitely worthwhile servitude because he is God, serving God.

Article 3.
Christ is also Lord through seigniory received over other human beings

622. Christ as man is the unique, faithful servant of God amongst human beings. In him, reverence and servitude towards the supreme Being are complete.

623. We have seen that faithful servitude towards God benefits only the one giving it, whose being is perfected and ennobled. Unfaithfulness in divine service has the opposite effect: it harms the unfaithful and wicked servant, whose being suffers harm and degeneration.

624. The unfaithful servant falls; the faithful servant is raised up. The whole human race, except Christ, failed in faithfulness. He is thus raised above all mankind.

[63] Is 49: 5.
[64] Ps 13: 3.

[617–624]

625. Consequently, God gave seigniory over the whole, unfaithful human family to Christ as man (upon whom the divine spirit had rested with all his gifts) because of his holiness. According to right, Christ could place mankind as a footstool under his feet, judge it, and strictly condemn it.[65]

Article 4.
Christ is also God's minister for the salvation of the world

626. But the Christ of God did not use his dominion to condemn the human family which he had at his disposition, although it had merited condemnation. The use of the dominion he had received was directed by two noble affections: 1. to use this dominion to give God once more the greatest possible service, by fulfilling perfectly his will; 2. to turn the dominion to redeeming from punishment human beings whom he loved as brethren in the equality of human nature he shared with them. He would achieve this by communicating something of his own holiness and divinity to them.

627. These two sublime affections were in perfect harmony. It was natural for Christ as man to show affection for his brethren, and it was the will of God that he should second this longing to benefit them. It was also the will of God that the dominion over mankind given to his faithful servant should result in the greatest satisfaction of that servant, as Isaiah says, 'THE WILL OF THE LORD SHALL PROSPER IN HIS HAND.'[66] On Christ's part, the work of redemption was therefore voluntary.

628. But it was also the fulfilment of a command received from God who wanted Christ to redeem mankind, his brethren, because this was required by Christ's natural love. Moreover, because God himself loved human beings as his creatures, and because the end of the universe had been obtained through the perfect servitude of his Christ, he wished it to be obtained in

[65] In Isaiah, God says of his Christ as man: 'Behold my servant, whom I uphold, my chosen in whom my soul delights; I have put my Spirit upon him, he will bring forth justice to the nations' (42: 1).

[66] Is 53: 10.

other human beings, Christ's brethren by nature, through the work of Christ.[67] On his side, Christ loved the will of God, which he knew perfectly, even more than he loved his brethren. It was his pleasure to carry out the design established by God from the constitution of the world. The work of redemption, therefore, was the accomplishment of the will of God.

Article 5.
Christ is also judge of the world, and head of the Church

629. Through his pre-eminent holiness Christ had obtained absolute dominion over guilty humanity, and authority to judge it. Through his suffering for human beings, which satisfied justice, and through the ransom of his blood, they became his property under the new title of redemption, so that he was able to communicate to them gifts and degrees of holiness as he pleased.[68] In this, too, he wanted to conform to the eternal design of God which was in fact ordered to the greatest glory and exaltation of Christ, the Redeemer whose now glorious natural will found itself perfectly attuned to such a design. From every point of view, as Isaiah had predicted so profoundly, 'the will of God would prosper in the hands of his Christ'.[69]

630. The human beings for whom Christ suffered remain divided between those who come to receive the benefit of his redemption, and those who do not. Relative to the second

[67] Isaiah notes that the servitude to be given to God by his Christ was to consist in the work of salvation applied to Hebrews and Gentiles. Christ says through the lips of the prophet: 'And now the Lord says, who formed me from the womb to be his servant, to bring Jacob back to him, and that Israel might be gathered to him, for I am honoured in the eyes of the LORD, and my God has become my strength.' He says: 'It is too light a thing that you should be my servant to raise up the tribes of Jacob and to restore the preserved of Israel; I will give you as a light to the nations, that my salvation may reach to the end of the earth' (Is 49: 5–6).

[68] Therefore it is said, 'When he ascended on high he led a host of captives, and he gave gifts to men' (Eph 4: 8).

[69] 'Yet it was the will of the LORD to bruise him; he has put him to grief; when he makes himself an offering for sin, he shall see his offspring, he has prolonged his days; the will of the LORD shall prosper in his hand' (Is 53: 10).

group, Christ's power is shown principally in the judgement which he will pronounce over them at the end; relative to those to whom the merit of his suffering is communicated, his power is manifested in the task he carries out as their head. With them he forms a tightly knit society, called *Church*, and it is of this society that we have to speak in expounding the governmental and communal right of theocratic society.

631. Only with the damned, therefore, does Christ exercise the right of mere dominion. With the members of his Church he exercises, as man, the rights of governor, fellow-member and benefactor.

SECTION TWO

GOVERNMENTAL RIGHT IN THEOCRATIC SOCIETY

632. We must now speak about these rights of Christ and, at the same time, see what part of them he has communicated to the Church, the theocratic society he founded.

First, we have to examine more carefully the nature of theocratic society. The definition given at the beginning of our study is no longer sufficient by itself to ensure clarity and order in a discussion of such rights.

The present section, therefore, will contain two chapters. In the first, we shall consider the nature of theocratic society at its differing levels of formation, but especially at the final level to which it has been raised by Christ. In the second, we shall investigate right in this society.

CHAPTER 1
The nature of theocratic society

633. Perfect theocratic society, that is, the Church of JESUS Christ, is simply the natural society of mankind raised in certain human beings to the supernatural order and brought to its final completion and full realisation.

634. Let us begin by viewing globally the traces of theocratic society presented by nature. We shall then see how the Redeemer, after taking up the primal design of the Creator, notwithstanding the devastation wrought in it by the sins of men and women, restored his work and brought it to completion without abandoning these traces, and raised theocratic society to its highest level on earth and in heaven.

[632–634]

Article 1.
The character of the natural society of mankind: the first
trace of true theocracy

635. Does mankind form a society by nature? This is the first
question springing to mind when serious thought is given to
government in theocratic society. In this chapter we shall
answer the question, and show that:

§1. *A society of mankind exists by nature*

636. Our heading does not refer to domestic society, which is
produced contemporaneously by human nature and human
activity. Because it is *produced*, it does not depend solely upon
the nature of things.

637. Our question asks whether human beings, by their
simple co-existence on earth, are joined in a *de iure* society,
inherent to their humanity.

638. I am speaking of a *de iure society*. I do not deny that an
external, *de facto society* corresponding to the *de jure* society
may either be lacking or in a deplorable state. A domestic
society may be torn apart by internal strife, for example; citizens
may be engaged in civil war. But despite the disunion and
struggle between members of these societies, forgetful of their
social obligations, the *right* which presides unchangeably over
domestic and civil society, and forms them, is not destroyed. In
so far as they exist by right, such societies are immune from
damage and unfailing. A natural society amongst human beings
has to be thought of in the same way. Although the obligations
it imposes may be left unfulfilled by human waywardness, and
men and women live unconscious of its existence, it continues
to be.[70]

---

[70] Persons capable of self-observation should note how many things exist
or arise in the human mind and heart without entering consciousness. This is
one of the facts of the human spirit which are easily overlooked, although
they are of extreme importance to the would-be philosopher. Cicero, for
example, observed the existence of a natural society of mankind, of which
human beings were often unconscious: 'As we use our limbs before we learn

639. Philosophers and historians of antiquity agree in affirming this.

Philosophers often speak of a universal society of mankind;[71] historians, in describing the history of their particular nations, often show them made up of wanderers thrown together in a life that was at least uncivilised, if not altogether unsocial [*App.*, no. 2]. St. Augustine summed up this two-fold condition of mankind when he said, 'There is nothing more viciously disagreeable nor more naturally social than mankind.'[72]

640. It is easy to recognise in mankind all the constitutive elements of society we have already explained. Hence we can affirm that the Creator, in placing mankind upon earth, posited with it an essential, co-created society which would precede all others, and be their foundation and support.

641. As we have said, every society is constituted by a *common good*, towards which the wills of several persons aim together in order that all may enjoy it or profit from it.

Every human being possesses connatural, identical rights, that is, rights having as their object three goods identical in all human beings: *truth*, *virtue* and *happiness*. (cf. *RI*, 84–244).

These three goods can never be the private and exclusive possession of any one person because they are inexhaustible and unlimited by time and space. Characteristically and essentially they are common to all (cf. *RI*, 390–391).

642. Because they are not subject to the laws of time and space, these intellectual and moral goods enjoy a property lacking in other so-called inexhaustible goods, such as light and air, which cannot be entirely appropriated by a single person, although they are limited and material (cf. *RI*, 392). Such goods can in fact be diminished by the use made of them by other human beings. Air, for instance, can be used up by a crowd in a room, or

the purpose for which they have been given us, so by nature we are united and associated in civil society' (*De Finib.*, 3). We need only note in this passage that Cicero confuses *civil society* with *natural* (theocratic) *society*. This is the result of absolutism in pagan civil society which, as we have said before, absorbed every other society, just as *civil right* imagined it could swallow up all other right.

[71] 'As far as I can see, it is obvious that we all come into existence forming a kind of society with one another' (Cic, *De Am.*, 5).

[72] *The City of God*, bk. 12, c. 27.

infected by people or clothes. Moreover, each individual enjoys only a part of these material, so-called inexhaustible objects and cannot enjoy another's part of them. On the other hand, intellectual and moral goods — truth, virtue and happiness — are:

1. *undiminishable*; that is, they are not decreased in relationship to individuals whatever the satisfaction obtained from them by other persons;

2. *indivisible*: each individual enjoys them in their integrity and totality, not as a separate part of a whole, although the totality itself can be enjoyed to different degrees by different individuals;

3. *identical*: these goods enjoyed identically by an individual of the human species can be enjoyed by all the other individuals of the species indefinitely and without limit.

643. In addition, the three goods we have indicated are proper to human nature.

Truth is inherent to human beings, and informs them;[73] *virtue* is the perfection of the human *person*;[74] *happiness* is the perfect state to which man's essential feeling tends incessantly (that is, a human being tends by nature to happiness because he is a substance-feeling, and the perfect state of feeling cannot be found outside virtue, the perfection of the person).[75]

644. All this, however, would not be sufficient to prove that there is by nature a universal society of mankind. The good which forms society must not only be common and public; it must be used in communion if a society is to exist. Solitary contemplatives could not be said to be united in a society if, while sharing in what is true and just, they ignored one another (cf. *USR*, 45).

This constitutive element is not lacking, however. Granted only that human beings know of their co-existence, we may affirm that the goods we have mentioned are, of their own nature and because of human nature, posited and enjoyed in communion.

645. In fact, *truth* unifies human individuals. It is nothing

[73] Ideal being, the form of human understanding, is *truth itself*. Cf. *CE*, 1112–1135.

[74] *ER*, 181–182.

[75] Cf. *SP*, 545–576.

more than the *idea* making known real things. But the idea, in so far as it makes man known, becomes the foundation of the human *species*. Every real human being is known through the same identical idea of human being, that is, ideal human nature, or human nature as knowable. Because a single, identical idea makes known all human individuals, the same identical realised essence, the same nature, is known in each of them. Consequently, all men and women are said to form a single human *species*. All intelligent beings, however, and this includes human beings, love things in the way in which they know them. Love proceeding from the subject receives its direction from the idea (the object). Granted the nature of the idea, it is clear that when we see a single thing, that is, a single nature in ourselves and in all other human beings and, as a result, love this nature, we come naturally to love all the individuals of our *species* as ourselves. This single love for all human beings sown in each by nature makes each one desire for the others the same good as he desires for himself. His supreme goods, however, are truth, virtue and happiness, which he naturally wishes to possess and enjoy in communion with all his fellows. Human nature longs for and tends towards these goods as its end. But the human nature which a human being loves is identical in himself and in all those sharing it with him. *Truth*, therefore, draws all human beings towards love of one another as a single entity,[76] and calls out to be enjoyed by human beings in communion.

646. *Virtue* produces the same effect. As *justice*, it respects equally all human beings because they have the same nature, and consequently wants the supreme goods of this nature to be common to all the individuals possessing it.[77] As *goodness*, it leads human beings to desire the supreme goods not for them-

---

[76] Hence the expression used by the head of humanity, the perfect man, when he prayed that human beings might find unity: 'THAT THEY MAY BE ONE THING'. (Jn 17: 11).

[77] Cicero (*De Legibus*, bk. 1) proves the existence of a natural society of mankind from the identity of right and justice; and he proves this identity from the identity of human nature, his starting point. 'We can distinguish good law from bad only by the rule given by NATURE; and it would be madness to say that such a rule depends upon what we think rather than upon NATURE' (c. 44). Hence he maintains that right between peoples is such by NATURE (*De Officiis*, bk. 3, c. 5, and elsewhere).

selves alone, but for the whole human race, and to encourage their common possession. No one would be virtuous who desired to have virtue for himself alone, or did not rejoice in having it in common with others, and in being able to love it with them and in them.

647. *Happiness* cannot be attained unless it is preceded by virtue, just as virtue is impossible if human beings do not accept truth as their escort. A person refusing to hold the supreme goods in human nature in communion with his fellows cannot be happy because he would no longer be reasonable or virtuous, and would in fact have already renounced truth and virtue.

648. Happiness consists in the love and enjoyment of good, and good is being. A person who does not love his fellows cannot be happy because he excludes from his love that part of being, and therefore of good, which he finds in them, thus depriving himself culpably of a part of good. This malicious and willed privation constitutes evil. Depriving oneself of the natural love of one's fellows means rejecting the good found in such love, which is such that Cicero, quoting Archita of Taranto, could say, 'If a human being were to ascend alone into the heavens, and from there admire the world of nature and the beauty of the stars, the wonder would mean nothing to him if he had no companion to listen to his comments.'[78] How true this is! The only qualification to be made about applying it to the possession of absolute good, which contains every good, is that absolute good, although it could certainly be enjoyed fully by an individual, could not be enjoyed by an individual wishing to be its sole possessor to the exclusion of others.[79]

---

[78] *De Amicitia*, 23. Seneca agrees: 'If wisdom were given on condition that it were to be kept hidden, I would reject it' (*Letters* 5).

[79] On the other hand, there is some good, or rather some form of enjoyment of what is good, that excludes the company of others. This depends upon the human instinct for being first and having a special place. Common good is desired, but not without some special, exclusive privilege in its enjoyment. Well-understood and correctly applied, this is not a defect, nor anything willed; it is dependent upon the nature of beings, and as such is an ontological law. For this reason God possesses something in himself that he does not and cannot communicate, and the saints themselves have been promised, besides the enjoyment common to all, some exclusive and special happiness: 'To him who conquers I will give some of the HIDDEN MANNA,

649. The unity and simplicity of the sublime goods to which human nature is directed gives unity to this nature, and constitutes in a natural society the real individuals in human nature. On the one hand, these goods are common by nature; on the other hand, they would cease to be if human beings, knowing one another, refused to possess them in common.

650. Another consequence is that truth, virtue and happiness can be said to be bonds between intelligent beings. Their very concept includes society between intelligences, which are *essentially* unitive and social.[80]

§2. *The threefold characteristic of natural theocratic society: unity, universality and justice*

651. *Unity*, *universality* and *justice* are the three characteristics of natural theocratic society.

652. Unity: theocratic society is one, as truth and justice are one.

653. Universality: theocratic society is universal because it sets before itself the supreme good of human nature, a good which is identical for all those belonging to this nature.

654. Justice: theocratic society is just because its very desire for justice gives it existence.

The sublime characteristics of these three supreme goods which form the object of pure-connatural rights shows that such goods are of their nature social to the highest degree. A society taking them as its aim is bound to excel, and to possess a singular degree of intimacy.

655. The *intimacy* of a society depends upon the intimacy of its *communion* in the good forming its object.

656. When *communion* is at its most intense,
   1. the object enjoyed by the members is perfectly *identical*;

and I will give him A WHITE STONE with A NEW NAME written on the stone which NO ONE KNOWS EXCEPT HIM WHO RECEIVES IT (Apoc 2: 17). Because this kind of enjoyment is unknown to others, it cannot be enjoyed by them. It is non-existent to them, and cannot be desired for them by others. Desiring them to share it would be a contradiction destroying it.

[80] For our comments on society as invisible, cf. *SP*, 235–262.

2. the object cannot be divided, but is so simple that it is given *whole* to all;

3. each person enjoys this unique, simple object to the extent of his capacity, and of his desire to satisfy his capacity.

657. Communion in any material good whatsoever lacks these conditions, and can never be as perfect as communion in intellectual and moral goods, which alone are suitable for constituting a society that draws its members into the intimacy of greatest union.

§3. *The society of mankind cannot be destroyed or replaced by any other society*

658. If the society of mankind, as we have described it above, is brought into being by nature, it is part of *socio-natural right*, and as such antecedent to positive right, which cannot destroy it.

659. No other society or legislation whatsoever can destroy or change the first, natural society of mankind without offending, violating and destroying human nature. Positive laws directed against the basic society of mankind are *per se* null.

Confirmation can be found in the following argument. The *supreme goods*, the aim of universal society, are the great and final object of human *rights* and *duties*.

In so far as mankind's greatest right lies in these goods, any attempt to violate them is an injury committed against mankind itself, harmed in its supreme, essential rights.

660. In so far as mankind's greatest duty lies in these goods, any attempt to deflect mankind from this society is a crime against all moral legislation.

§4. *Every other society is subordinate to the society of mankind*

661. Every other society formed by human beings is therefore guilty and evil if it does not respect the primal human society and acknowledge its laws as inviolable.

[657–661]

Every society dependent upon human initiative is subordinate to and dependent upon primal, universal society.

§5. *The universal society of mankind is the first nucleus of every other society; every other society must aim at perfecting and completing it*

662. The goods proper to universal society are supreme goods, rooted in absolute good, and cannot be renounced by human nature, which would have no final end without them. Consequently every other society must have as its *remote end* the same good as universal society, from which it can differ only in reference to its *proximate end*. The *proximate end* itself must be desired as a means of obtaining the remote end.[81]

663. No good falls within the *absolute notion* of good unless it is destined to increase true human good, that is, virtue and happiness. Other societies must aim finally at the realisation and fulfilment of the end of human society. This society is the nucleus of all other societies which legitimately draw together human beings.

§6. *Universal society is bonded by universal love*

664. Nevertheless, it often happens that *particular*, artificial *societies* are unashamedly opposed to natural, *universal* society.

665. There are two principle reasons for this.

First, particular societies have relative, partial good as their aim. Universal society is directed towards ultimate, total good. If members of a particular society love excessively and exclusively the good that forms its proximate end, they will not order and submit it to the good of universal society, the remote end it must serve. In this way, love of finite things often wages war against truth and virtue, which are infinite goods.

666. The second reason is that the membership of particular societies is limited numerically, while universal society embraces

[81] Cf. *SP*, 204–210.

all human beings. The bond of particular societies is special love of family, city or so-called public domain; the bond of universal society is the universal love of mankind called *humanity* or, to use St. Paul's Greek word, *philanthropy*.[82] Every time special love expands and seeks absolute status, it excludes universal love. Particular societies thus become inhuman and as such hostile to universal love amongst human beings, and adversaries of their own natural society.

667. If particular societies are not to endanger universal society, they have to submit to two laws:

1. No particular society is to seek absolutely and unconditionally the special good at which it aims. It must do so moderately, that is, relatively to the supreme good of universal society, which it will prefer to its own special good when a clash occurs between them.

2. A particular society's love for its members may not detract from or restrict universal love for all men. On the contrary, it must further it. All love of family, country or any other society whatsoever is to be founded in common love, and is to be at the service of the universal love of humanity embracing every human individual.

§7. *The universal society of mankind is the design for theocratic society*

668. We have illustrated the nature, splendid gifts and sublime prerogatives of the natural society of the human race. Such teaching is already sufficient to enable us to form the concept of what we have called theocratic society, because mankind's first, natural society is an outline, still to be fleshed out, of theocratic society.

669. Let us ask ourselves again: what is theocratic society? It is society at its highest level, where human beings and God have the same good, which they share and enjoy in communion.

Pagan philosophers themselves recognised expressly that mankind's natural society implies society between mankind and God.

[82] Cf. Tit 3: 4.

The great sages, who truly merited the name of philosophers, recognised truth and virtue as divine goods in which God and human beings intercommunicate.

670. Cicero admirably develops on platonic lines this truly noble thought. Seeking for a solid basis of civil laws, he finds it in the natural society of the human race, and recognises that this natural society involves a kind of society with God himself. This is how he describes the theocratic character of human society:

> What is more divine in the whole of heaven and earth, man included, than reason? Developed and perfected, it is rightly called wisdom. But because there is nothing better than reason, and reason is found in both man and in God, man forms an initial society of reason with God. Those with reason in common, however, have right reason, that is, law, in common. We must affirm, therefore, that human beings are associated with the gods through law. But those with law in common also possess communion of rights. Having these things in common means existing as members of the same city. Because it obeys the same laws and authorities, and especially when it obeys the heavenly rules of the all-powerful, divine mind, the entire world[83] has to be thought of as a single city common to God and human beings. What happens in civil society, where agnation is the rule for distinguishing states, occurs also, but at a much higher level, in the nature of things: human beings consider themselves agnate descendants of the gods.[84]

Article 2.
The character of realised, fulfilled theocratic society, that is, of the Christian Church

§1. *Its notion*

671. Nevertheless, the natural society of mankind is theocratic society in outline only. The design still lacks the realisation that

---

[83] Here we should perhaps read: *et iam universus hic mundus* instead of *ut iam universus hic mundus.* The error would have crept in as time went by.

[84] *De Legibus*, 1, 7.

posits the society it initiates in perfect being. This realisation can be brought about by God alone, through the supernatural communication of himself to human beings and by the consequent communion of his very own goods with them. It is worthwhile illustrating this briefly from various points of view already indicated in our previous publications.

672. The truth naturally manifested to our soul is something divine, but not God himself. Pagan philosophers who thought of it in this way can be excused, because it was the only divine element to be found in the whole universe. But God himself has been communicated to Christians, who are able to compare the light of reason with the light of faith. The comparison enables us to discern easily the difference between *God*, to whom we are joined supernaturally by faith, and the simple *idea* (truth) to which we are joined by nature.[85]

673. The difference can best be understood by first noting accurately that every being can be communicated to us under two forms, which I have called *ideal form* and *real form*. However, we do not normally say that an entity has been truly communicated to us if it has been communicated only in its *ideal*, and not in its *real form*. The *subsistence* of a being lies in its real form, which we have defined as 'the real act by which the essence of a thing exists', and, as we have said, 'essence is that which is manifested in the idea'.[86] If the idea of food had been communicated to us, we definitely would not say that food had been communicated to us. The idea of food allows us to know the possibility of food, the essence of food, but until food has acted upon us in its subsistence it would not be communicated to us. In order that a being communicate itself (in its subsistence)

---

[85] Arguments for this important distinction may be examined in *Rinnovamento* etc. bk. 3, c. 62, and *La Storia Comparativa de' Sistemi Morali*, c. 6. — To say that the *being* we intuit by nature is God would lead to most serious consequences. In fact, we predicate *being* of everything, including that which is contingent. Hence, we would predicate God of these things also. But if God can be predicated of all things, all entities, then everything is God, and we fall inevitably into pantheism, a doctrine far removed from what we maintain. To say, 'What is divine can only be God', implies incapacity to grasp that the distinction between the divine and God is relative to us alone; it does not entail any kind of distinction or separation in God.

[86] Cf. *OT*, 646.

[672–673]

to us, it must communicate itself in its *real form*. In this form, it does not communicate itself to the mind enlightened by the idea, but to the feeling, by working with its reality in our own reality. If we have the idea of food, and food itself is really present and working upon our senses so that we can see, touch and taste it, etc., then we say that it is truly communicated to us. Let us apply the same distinction to God.

God is being in its fullness, but as long as *being* communicates itself to us only in its ideality it does not communicate itself in its fullness, which requires both forms. It is not correct, therefore, to say that God communicates himself to us in the natural light of the intellect: 1. because in God the ideal form cannot be divided from the real form without the destruction for us of the divine being, to which fullness and absoluteness are essential; 2. because even if the division were possible, ideal being would be insufficient to communicate to us the being itself which it enables us to know.

In fact, one cannot rightly say that being in its ideal form is the idea of God because there is no (positive) *idea* of God. If there were, it would express a possible God. A possible God, however, is not God because subsistence is essential to God. God in real form cannot be separated from God in ideal form. In God, these forms are absolutely undivided. Human beings, who have been given being in its ideal form, have not been given God.

674. Hence (essential) being is communicated to us by nature in its ideal form only. This constitutes the *natural order*. Being itself is shown to us in the fullness of its *real form* through grace, a true communication and perception of God, which constitutes the supernatural order.

675. The distinction between the two orders eliminates *rationalism*, which reduces everything to natural reason, that is, to the idea; it also eliminates the contrary error of *mysticism*, which asserts that human beings by nature are in communication with the reality of God.

676. The supernatural order, therefore, is constituted by a real communication of God to man. God, with his grace, works in the substance of the human soul. Because the soul consists entirely of feeling, the effect of the supernatural communication is a *deiform feeling* of which initially we have no consciousness,

just as we have no consciousness of any substantial, fundamental feeling of our own.[87]

677. The *deiform feeling* of which we are speaking has its
beginning in this life, in which it constitutes the light of *faith* and
of *grace*; and its completion in the next life, in which it constitutes the light of *glory*.

678. Granted these notions, it is easy to deduce that in the
natural order theocratic society is only outlined because the idea
is the rule of good, but not itself real good.[88] In the supernatural
order, theocratic society is complete because the *good* which it
possesses and intends to enjoy is God, *full ideal-real* being.

It will help if we list more carefully the successive grades of
perfection that can be conceived in theocratic society amongst
humans, beginning from its most imperfect state.

§2. *The different levels of perfection according to which theocratic society can be considered*

679. Constitutive elements in every society are
 1. the common good;
 2. the communion in which the common good is enjoyed.
Theocratic society, the society which human beings form with
God, is therefore more perfect in so far as
 1. the common good between human beings and God is
greater;
 2. the communion in which this good is possessed and
enjoyed is more intimate.

680. It is not difficult to deduce from these two criteria the
states or levels of varying perfection that can be thought of in
theocratic society.

I.
The first level of theocratic society — human reason alone

681. First, we realise that natural, human society, is the most

[87] *Ibid.* 715–719.
[88] *CE*, 1234–1236.

imperfect state of all. It is an outline of theocratic society rather than its first level.

682. In this state the common good (the first constitutive element) is truth, ideal being.

But ideal being, unaccompanied by the reality of being, is the least of divine goods for mankind. To demonstrate this, it is sufficient to recall what we have said elsewhere.[89]

683. Man's perfection is moral perfection. Moral good consists in adhering with one's entire self to the totality of being, of which ideal being is only one form.

How do human beings adhere to being in its form as truth?

They take it simply as a *rule*, according to which they have to direct their longings and actions. Because *ideal being* is only the means of knowledge, (that is, the light manifesting the essences of things,[90]) it is simply that by which we know the various degrees of being contained in these essences; it is the norm according to which our willed acknowledgement of every being is directed. But *ideal being* has no other function, and we have to love, respect and obey it only in so far as it carries out this noble function of enlightening and directing our will and our feeling.

684. If the entire function of ideal being consists in directing our activity, it requires something other than itself. Its value is relative to the beings it enables us to know and to which it leads us so that we may adhere to them in an orderly fashion, as we should. Let us consider its value in the order of nature.

Within the circle of nature, *ideal being* can lead us to adhere only to natural things, to limited and finite beings. It is true that it leads us to do this in right order so that amongst these beings we give preference to what should be preferred. For example, we give preference to a human being rather than a horse, and consider a horse on a lower level than a human being. But in the last analysis, we are dealing in nature with finite beings. Virtue will be present, but virtue having as its object a finite being — for example, man. Humanity, friendship, and so on, will be present, but nothing more. This virtue is necessarily imperfect

[89] Cf. *Storia comparativa de' Sistemi Morali*, c. 8, art. 3, §7.
[90] Cf. our definition of essence: 'Essence is that which is seen in the idea' (*OT*, 646).

(in so far as it can be put into practice) because its object is finite;
all virtue is reduced to acknowledging the order of being within
the sphere of the finite. But because this virtue is imperfect,
actual adherence to truth is also imperfect. Our greater adherence to truth depends on our acknowledging it in a wider
sphere of real objects whose value and order is revealed by truth
itself. We adhere to *truth* through *virtue*; we adhere to truth
when we adhere to real beings according to the order indicated
in them by truth itself.

Now, God is his own good. He loves truth in acknowledging
himself; he loves it infinitely because he loves it in the sphere of
the infinite. He loves creatures in himself, in the creating act
where the strength of their subsistence lies. The love which God
has towards creatures does not increase or diminish in him his
love for himself, nor does this love really differ from love of
himself. Without the love of his creatures (granted that these
have been willed by him in their subsistence and hence created)
he would not love himself. What common good, therefore, is
found between God and human beings constituted within the
limits of nature?

The *real good* loved by human beings, and the real good loved
by God, is essentially different because God's good is himself,
while the real good of human beings is created good. These
goods are essentially different; no society is present because
there is no communion in good. Nevertheless, an opening exists
through which humans can arrive at communion of good if God
draws them to it. The created good can be loved in itself, or
loved in its source, in God. It cannot, however, be loved in God
if God is not loved first. If, therefore, God draws human beings
to himself by communicating himself to them, created good can
be loved by them in God and thus become a good common to
God and human beings. Properly speaking, there is no communion with created good alone. There is only a passive power, or
capacity, for such communion, which cannot be the foundation
of society.

685. *Ideal being* remains as something certainly common to
natural man and to God, but at an infinite distance. The beauty
and lovableness of ideal being springs from its relationship with
real being, whose essence and intrinsic order it reveals. As long
as human beings are in contact with real finite being alone, ideal

being is loved and appreciated in a finite manner. This explains why the Gentiles could never in practice consider justice and moral good as superior to all transitory goods.

686. It is true that ideas (laws and rules of what is just) can be contemplated speculatively by means of a ray of infinite beauty, but this is altogether inadequate for producing in our reality a corresponding love, which can only be roused by another reality working within us. Plato was right when he said of wisdom, 'If it could be seen, it would stimulate wonderful love for itself'.[91] Because platonic wisdom is reduced to virtue, Cicero applied these words to the beauty of decency and justice.[92] Wisdom, in fact, depends upon the intellect's intuition of truth; virtue consists in adhering with the will to the truths known by the intellect; and the truth to which human beings adhere becomes known as wisdom. But the sages of antiquity saw that the idea alone without the thing it indicated had no power to move man, a real substance, to action. Cicero speaks of this explicitly, 'In all that we do, we are moved not by word, but by reality'.[93]

687. The common good, the first constitutive element of society, is barely present in the natural order if we compare it with what God and human beings could have in common. What is the situation with regard to the second constitutive element?

What kind of communion in good is found between God and human beings?

This depends upon the possibilities of what we call *natural*

---

[91] Cf. *Phaedrus*.

[92] *De Officiis*, bk. 1, c. 5: 'Mark, my son, you behold the form itself which you see as the expression of what is decent. If your eyes could penetrate it, wonderful love for it would be aroused, as Plato says.'. Pearcio's suggestion that the text should be corrected to read: 'as Plato says about wisdom', is untenable. He did not realise that in Plato wisdom and decency can be taken as synonymous.

[93] The complete text is as follows: 'Our eyes are a very sharp sense in us BUT WE DO NOT PENETRATE TO WISDOM THROUGH THEM (people felt the need to perceive wisdom in its reality). Wisdom would indeed stimulate such burning affection for itself if it WERE SEEN! (that is, if it were perceived not only ideally, but really). Why? Because it is so warm that it can excite the desires? Why do we praise justice? And what about that ancient proverb: everyone is in darkness? In a word, it is perfectly clear that in everything we do we are moved by what is real, not by ideas' (*De Finibus*, 2: 16).

religion. Reason can certainly argue to the existence of a God who loves truth and virtue but, although logically necessary in itself, such reasoning has little effect in producing living persuasion and operative faith in what lies beyond the senses, although it boldly surpasses the confines of the universe and, by virtue of the principles of *integration* and *absolute subsistence*,[94] penetrates the invisible and infinite.

688. There have been atheists in every age of history. What they lack is not *proof* of God's existence, but the *persuasion* that makes people assent to proof. The best of pagan philosophers have hesitated over the question of the immortality of the soul and the existence of another world. As Cicero says, he believed in immortality as long as he was reading the *Phaedo*, but doubted about the arguments as soon as he put the book down. In the same dialogue, which can be considered the final achievement of Greek thought (and how uncertain and hesitant it is!), Socrates shows clearly that he wants to persuade people of the existence of the world to come by suggestions, rather than argue to it rigorously [*App.*, no. 3]. Kant, in turn, was discouraged enough to abandon theoretical reason, when he saw it presented no argument powerful enough to lead to a conclusion about the existence of God. His rejection of all theoretical proofs of God's existence was copied by one author after another in Germany, and has been echoed in Italy.

689. Why do these intellectual proofs demonstrating the existence, reason and origin of a world beyond what is visible have no power to impel a strong, undoubting assent from so many when they seem to me rigorous in the extreme? Because although they have their origin in *ideal being*, the source of the *principles* on which they rest, ideal being alone has very little operative power over man, a real subject, and hence does not always produce persuasion within him. Persuasion is not an *idea*, but a *reality*, a real act, a feeling of a real being.[95]

690. We conclude that communion in good (in truth) between human beings and God is only tenuously present in the order of nature. Communion is lacking between members of a society if

---

[94] Cf. *CE*, 1460.

[95] On the very important distinction between *persuasion* and the *intuition of truth*, cf. *CE*, 1040–1042.

the members neither know one another, nor know the common good, nor desire to enjoy it together. But, in the order of nature, human beings have an ineffective persuasion of the God whom they know in a certain way only. Moreover, it is difficult for them to consider him as a moral God, loving the truth and virtue in which he delights. In this state, man's appreciation and evaluation of truth and virtue are very imperfect. Practically speaking, at least in the long term, man does not place such goods above all others.

It follows that communion in good, the second constitutive element of society, is to be found between man and God at its most imperfect level in the natural order where the theocratic society possesses only an incipient grade of perfection.

II.
The second level of theocratic society — revelation

691. Natural theocratic society, or embryo of society, is elevated to a higher grade when God, acting in wonderful ways, positively manifests to human beings the truth of his existence and his holiness of being, which makes him delight and rejoice in truth and justice.

692. These positive proofs of the existence of an infinite and eternal Being and his sublime attributes, point to another life where evil is punished and good rewarded. They consolidate *persuasion* of these truths, and thus strengthen *communion in good* (the second constitutive element of society).

693. The *common good* itself (the first constitutive element of society) is not increased, however, nor enhanced, unless God adds to the *revelation* he makes to human beings the interior communication called *grace*. Without grace, the common good remains at the level of *ideal being*, at the level of truth naturally possessed by human beings, and at the level of consequent natural virtue.

III.
The third level of theocratic society — grace

694. On the other hand, God may communicate the gift of his

grace to the human spirit, in addition to a *revelation* which provides positive proofs of his existence, holiness and justice in rewarding good and punishing evil. If so, theocratic society receives a new, highly uplifting impulse.

695. Through grace the *common good* between mankind and God is completed, and in reaching completion changes its character. It is no longer merely ideal being; it is now God himself, ideal-real being.

696. The word 'grace', as we understand it here, indicates a real communication made by God of himself to human beings. God gives himself to human beings by means of an interior, hidden work; he gives himself to intimate, human feeling. Through grace, human beings have the feeling of God, and the faculty for acting according to this divine feeling. As we have often said, every feeling produces of itself an instinct, or activity.[96]

697. By 'feeling of God' or 'deiform feeling', we understand a feeling whose nature is such that it shows itself to the person reflecting upon it as a felt action of God. As an effect it is felt in such a way that it cannot be attributed to any finite cause, but only to the infinite cause. Properly speaking, it makes us *perceive God*,[97] (that is, God's immediate action in us); it does not enable us to *argue* to God.

IV.
The fourth level of theocratic society: the Incarnation,
in which theocratic society reaches its perfection

698. A direct action of God in the substance of the human soul, where it produces a deiform fundamental feeling, raises man above the natural order and places him in the supernatural state. This action, which is God himself (because the immediate action of God is God) puts human beings in immediate communication with God; it makes them perceive God. God as felt, as perceived, is the supreme common good between God and

[96] Cf. *AMS*, 367–369.

[97] For *perception* as founded in the feeling of the action of things upon us, and how it provides us with positive knowledge of these things, cf. *CE*, 1219–1244.

man, and brings theocratic society to its completion. Nevertheless, this society, which has thus passed from an embryonic to a completed state, may still receive another, finally perfecting touch.

699. God, who is most simple and perfect, cannot be perceived piecemeal; he can only be perceived in his totality. However, limited being, while perceiving him as *all* cannot, as the theologians say, perceive him *wholly*. The *object* of perception is unlimited, but the *mode* of perception remains limited. Yet God, who is his own absolute good in which he finds bliss, wished to put himself in communion with human beings not only by bestowing on them the perception of the *all* but, with a decree worthy of his divine attributes, by doing this as completely as possible. How can we come to grips with such a problem and such a profound mystery?

700. The divine mind purposed the Incarnation, by which God in the entirety of his substance would be joined to man in the person of the Word. What happened as a result?

The inevitable occurred. In the composite effected between man and the Word, God as infinitely greater had to prevail and himself alone remain as *person*. The human person vanishes because the supreme principle of the human nature assumed by the Word ceases to be supreme, and so ceases to be person. Person, as we have defined it, is 'a substantial, intelligent individual, in so far as the individual contains a supreme, active and incommunicable principle.'[98] In the God-man, the *supreme principle* alone is *divine*. In Christ, therefore, there is only one person, a divine person. The situation was necessarily overturned. The total communication of God to man required this; instead of man's assuming God, which was impossible, God came to assume man; he became man; he came to assume the whole of human nature and every part of human nature, including the flesh, through the unity of his personal principle. God became flesh; *et Verbum caro factum est*.[99]

701. As far as possible, human nature possessed the divine nature totally, but in the sense that the divine nature possessed human nature as its own, and possessed it in subsisting as a

[98] Cf. *AMS*, 832–837.
[99] Jn 1: 14.

divine person. The total possession of God by human nature consisted in the total possession of human nature by the divine person. The divine person possessed human nature as his very own.

702. In Christ, therefore, theocratic society between God and mankind reached and, we could say, even surpassed its fullness of perfection because:

1. The *common good* between God and man in the Incarnate Word is the greatest possible. In other words, all the good possessed by God is placed in communion with man, understood in the following sense: Christ as God, possessing the divinity as his Father does, consequently possesses all the good the Father has. As Scripture says, 'And all my things are yours, and yours are mine'.[100] These words express the greatest communion in good, and greatest society. If Christ possesses all this as God, the same can be said about his humanity, according to the communication of idioms, as theologians rightly put it. That is to say, what belongs to the divine nature is attributed to the human nature, and vice-versa, through the intimate, ineffable union joining them in a single person.

703. 2. *Communion* in this good is also at its height because the *good* enjoyed by God and man, the members of this society, is not a third thing, but the members themselves: God and all that he has; man and all that he has. In this union the Word enjoys the divinity and the humanity as his very own natural goods; man too enjoys the identical divinity and humanity as his very own goods. If the good were distinct from the members themselves, they could enjoy it separately, without knowing anything of one another; but if the members are this good, they can only enjoy each other, or rather each can enjoy both, in the most intimate communion. The order of communion is as follows. The good of human nature and that of divine nature are held in common; the greatest good of the society is the divine nature possessed by Father and Son and enjoyed as such. Christ, therefore, can say continually, 'We are one'.[101] The Son delights in this nature in the Father, the source from which he has received it; the Father delights in it in the Son, to whom he has

[100] Jn 17: 10.
[101] Jn: [10: 30].

communicated it through generation. But the person of the Son, having united human nature to himself, loves it and enjoys it from eternity. The Father cannot delight in the Son without delighting in the human nature of the Son because this nature possesses his Son in so far as it is possessed by him. The Father, therefore, can say, 'This is my beloved Son, in whom I am well-pleased: listen to him'.[102] He is speaking of delight in the divine person of the Son, which then descends to the Son's human nature in which and through which Christ exercises his office as legislator and teacher of human beings.

§3. *Christ draws other human beings into perfect theocratic society*

I.
The possession that man can have of God consists in being possessed by God

704. The greatest communication of himself made to man by infinite good consists in the possession taken of man by God. This reached its height in the Incarnation where the divine person was the supreme, operative principle in the composite. Human nature lost its personal principle because it no longer retained any supreme principle. All the human principles of action were subordinated to the divine principle, which directed and dominated them as its own.

705. Christ, the divine person who communicates the divinity to the human nature joined with him, also communicates the perception of the divinity to the other individuals of the human species through baptism and the grace of faith. In this way, Christ realises in himself the most perfect society between God and man, and draws other human beings into the same society.

706. These other human beings retain their personality because they are not individuated with the divine person who, however, while exercising the fullest dominion over them, does not destroy, but strengthens their freedom.

---

[102] 2 Pet 1: 17.

707. Complete theocratic society gradually forms itself around Christ, the divine person who assumed human nature, in this way:

1. The divine person, by means of the human nature he has assumed, communicates perception of the divinity to human persons with an interior action which, received in them, is called *grace*.

2. This infinite, feelable action enables human beings to perceive the divinity, and feel themselves obliged to submit fully to its dominion, wherein lies every good.

3. If humans do not reject this dominion but co-operate as adults with grace, God continues his sanctifying action, and directs all their actions according to the words, 'The Lord conducts the just through right ways;'[103] 'Abide in me, and I in you. I am the vine, you are the branches. He who abides in me, and I in him, he it is that bears much fruit, for apart from me you can do nothing'.[104] In these words, Christ expresses the *communion* of good between himself and those belonging to him; they must abide in him, he in them. But he also commands them, 'Abide in me', indicating that their consent, the co-operation of their will, is necessary, because every society requires voluntary consent (cf. *USR*, 34–36). Although human beings can do nothing in the supernatural order without Christ, they can do evil by freely rejecting grace, just as they can accept it when Christ, solely out of his infinite goodness, posits it in their souls.

708. The true interior and exterior society between human beings and God is proclaimed, therefore, only in the time of grace, through the society between Christ and human beings, whom he rightly calls his *friends* because he has placed in communion with them divine wisdom itself, as he said, 'All that I have heard from my Father I have made known to you'.[105] St. Paul could write to the Corinthians, 'God is faithful, by whom you were called into the society of his Son JESUS Christ, our Lord',[106] and St. John, announcing the things he had seen and heard, could write of this society to the faithful, 'so that you

[103] Wis 10: 10.
[104] Jn 15: 4–5.
[105] Jn 15: 15.
[106] 1 Cor 1: 9.

may have society with us; and OUR SOCIETY IS WITH THE FATHER
AND HIS SON JESUS CHRIST'.[107]

709. We conclude that perfect theocracy is realised not only in
Christ but through Christ in other human beings whom he
co-incorporates to himself by placing his divinity in communion with them to dominate in them as it does in him.

II.
The supreme dominion of God is identified with perfect theocratic society

710. All that we have noted conforms exactly with what we
said above about divine seigniory benefiting the servants, not
the Lord (cf. 579–585).

711. God's full dominion in the human being, that is, in the
will (where human personship lies) constitutes the only way in
which human beings can possess and enjoy God, the highest
good. God cannot be possessed except as he is — and he is
supreme Lord. Man, in possessing God acknowledges him as
such, annihilating himself beneath him, in order to taste and
enjoy what God is essentially, that is, Lord of creatures by
essence. No one can benefit from that essence except by delighting in God's absolute, infinite seigniory, and in the power he
exercises in the very substance of his creatures by the communication of himself. For this reason, theocratic society is also
called, most suitably, the KINGDOM OF GOD.

712. In considering the human side in such a society, we
rightly say that communion in the highest good, when present,
is accompanied by a society of service, submission and worship.
Such service and submission is the only thing (cf. *USR*, 141)
human beings have in common with one another but not with
God in this society, although it is possible to say, through the
communication of idioms, that God in Christ serves and renders worship to himself. God, however, in acknowledging himself, renders himself honour by glorifying himself; men render
him honour by humbling themselves.

[107] Jn 1: 3.

III.

Is the theocracy brought together by the Redeemer
a society of action or a society of fruition?

713. Nevertheless, in the present life Christ does not communicate clearly to others the perception of his divinity. The
light he gives is veiled; faith is necessary. In this state, theocratic
society is called *the Church militant* because in faith it fights the
Angel of Darkness who endeavours to destroy the Holy City.

714. *Living faith* is the principle of good works, and of the
eternal glory in which God is perceived unveiled.

Glory is the great term to which perfect theocratic society
tends, and where it attains its final perfection. In this state,
theocratic society is called *the Church triumphant*.

715. Theocratic society, therefore, considered as attaining
glory, is a society for enjoyment; considered as still travelling
and battling in this life, it is a society of both *fruition* and *action*.

716. Even here on earth Christ's society is a *society of fruition*.
It cannot be otherwise if in it, God, the essential good, is
communicated to human beings; he cannot be possessed without being enjoyed. Christ said, 'Come to me, all who labour and
are heavy laden, and I will give you rest.'[108] Moreover, his society
is blessed with hope.[109]

It is also a *society of action*. In the present life human beings
have to act to merit their reward; they have to trade with their
talents, conquer the enemy, increase their possession of God
until the moment they pass to the other life. Only then will the
effort of action cease and give way to unbroken fruition in the
life of peace defined by St. Augustine as 'THAT MOST ORDERLY
AND HARMONIOUS SOCIETY IN WHICH WE ENJOY GOD, AND ONE
ANOTHER IN GOD.'[110]

[108] Mt 11: 28.

[109] Speaking about the present life St. Augustine says: 'Although people
may possess this life in such a way that they refer its use to its end, which they
love most ardently and hope most faithfully, they can without absurdity be
called 'blessed' relative TO THEIR HOPE RATHER THAN TO THIS PRESENT LIFE'
(*The City of God*, 19: 20).

[110] *The City of God*, 19: 23.

IV.
A twofold theocratic society: of human beings with God,
and between human beings

717. From what has been said, we may infer that it is possible to distinguish, as it were, two intimately connected societies: that of human beings with God, and that between baptised people.

718. The society of baptised human beings with God is similar to that between children and their father (parental society); the society between the baptised resembles that between brothers and sisters having the same father (fraternal society).

719. In both societies, the good placed in common is the paternal patrimony; the children enjoy it, but the father owns and distributes it.

720. If we merely consider human beings living on earth, the distinction between their society with God and their society with one another is based on the variety of what has been placed in common.

721. Earthly sojourners, and God, have the divinity in common; it has to be acknowledged (virtue) and enjoyed (happiness).

But the wayfarers also have in common the power to merit with new, free actions that obtain for them greater right, and greater possession of the enjoyment of the divinity.

722. Human society with God is always a society of fruition. The theocratic society of action is that between human beings living on this earth.

This society is nevertheless rightly called theocratic not only because it possesses the good towards which it tends in hope, but also because God co-operates with his grace in human works and merits.

Christ said to Mary Magdalene, 'I am ascending to my Father and to your Father, to my God and to your God.'[111] With these words he shows that the good placed in communion is the Father, God, but he does not speak of 'our Father' nor 'our God' in order to indicate that God was his Father and his God

[111] Jn 20: 17.

[717–722]

in a way different from that in which he is Father and God of other human beings. He is Christ's Father by nature, not by adoption; and as his God, he is to be enjoyed. Christ no longer tends towards God meritoriously as pilgrims here on earth still have to do.

V.
The first three marks of theocratic society:
it is one, holy and catholic

723. If we consider the two societies as a single, resultant society, we can note certain of its very general marks.

The first, most general marks of theocratic society can only be those essential to the natural society of mankind, which we have already examined (cf. 651–654). The Church, as we said, is simply the society of mankind realised and completed by Christ.

The essential marks of the society of mankind are three: unity, justice and universality (cf. 651).

724. Christ himself unfolds the marvellous *unity* of his Church with words indicating the intense intimacy of the members of his mystical body with himself and contemporaneously amongst themselves.[112]

725. Moreover, in vivifying the Church with his Spirit, he gave the Church justice, indeed all justice, perfect and lasting *holiness*. He gave it not only natural justice, but the justice which consists principally in fulfilment of the precepts related to a God substantially communicated to man. In other words, he bestows on human beings a share in God's holiness.[113]

726. Finally, Christ called all human beings to himself,[114] and sent his disciples to all nations alike. The first teachers of the Church, therefore called her 'universal' or '*catholic*'.[115]

---

[112] Jn 17: 19–23; 10: 16. 'One Church throughout the whole world in many different members' (St. Cyprian, d. 258 AD, *Letter* 52).

[113] Acts 2: [33].

[114] 'Come to me, all of you' (Mt 11: 28; 28: 18–20).

[115] St. Ignatius of Antioch (d. 110 AD) already speaks of καθολικη εκκλησια (*Letter to the Church of Smyrna*, c. 8).

VI.
The invisible and visible parts of theocratic society

727. We can also apply to theocratic society the distinction made between *invisible* and *visible society*.[116]

According to this distinction, theocratic society amongst human beings is *invisible* and *visible*.

728. The *invisible* society is more extensive than the visible because it embraces both those who remain united to the *body* of the Church and those united only with its *spirit*.

729. The invisible society extends to those possessing the vision of heavenly glory; it is a society of fruition.

730. The visible society lives and fights upon earth.

VII.
The Church militant is a perfect society

731. The visible, hierarchic, militant Church, animated by an invisible spirit, constitutes of itself a perfect society whose invisible head is JESUS Christ. He governs it partly by his invisible grace and divine influence, and partly through his visible ministers who make up the hierarchy on earth.

732. United in spirit with the Church militant are the Church triumphant and the Church in *purgatory* (so called because its members, who have departed this life, must be cleansed and adorned to be worthy of entering the Church triumphant). These two parts of the Church are not visibly represented on earth, nor do they depend on the visible government of the Church militant. They are ruled only by their invisible head.

733. This does prevent the visible Church from being a perfect society, because it contains within itself all that is required to constitute a true, invisible society clothed in visible form. If we abstract mentally from the other two parts belonging only to the invisible society, the Church, although cut off from many of its noblest members, is not deprived of any element necessary for its constitution as a perfect society.[117]

[116] *SP*, 235–282.

[117] Hence Bellarmine on the Church militant: 'The Church is a society of

VIII.
The Church is different from every other society, including civil society

734. Because the Church militant is a theocratic society which exists *per se*, it differs from every other society, including civil society.

735. The community of the faithful differs therefore from the community formed by citizens, who may not be part of the assembly of the faithful; the ruling body presiding within the community of the faithful differs from that presiding over the community formed by citizens; the communities differ in their end. The Church, therefore, is not the nation, the nation is not the Church; the diocese is not the civil province; the parish is not the municipality. The Church therefore has rights distinct from those of civil society, or the State; and the State has rights distinct from those of the Church.

CHAPTER 2

Governmental right in perfect theocratic society

Article 1.
Governmental power *de facto*, and governmental power *de jure*, in the theocratic society founded by Christ

736. So far we have outlined the character of theocratic society, and examined the four levels by which it rises to its full being in the Redeemer. We must now set out the nature of its

human beings, not of angels, and not of souls. But it cannot be called a society of human beings if it is not set up with visible signs. There is no society which cannot be recognised by those who are its members, and the Church cannot be recognised by human beings if the bonds of the society are not visible and external. — St. Augustine says: "Human beings cannot be brought together in the name of any religion, true or false, unless they are under the banner of visible signs, that is, sacraments" (*Contra Faustum*, bk. 19, c. 2)' (*De Ecclesia Militante*, bk. 3, c. 12).

government, and the right bestowed upon it for its suitable
direction.

We need to keep clearly in mind the distinction between the
power of *dominion*, of which we have spoken, and the *governmental power* of which we have to speak. Simple dominion is
extended even over those who are not members of the theocratic
society, or have renounced membership, and over inanimate
creatures.

737. We must note, however, that all divine dominion, in
creating, conserving and disposing all things, is ruled by infinite
wisdom and providence, which guides its exercise for the good
of the theocratic society.

738. Moreover, both the power of divine seigniory and governmental power can be considered under two aspects: as a *fact*,
or as a *right*.

739. What is the *de facto* power in the theocratic society of
Christianity?

We saw that this society is founded in the hidden action
exercised by God himself in the substance of the intellective
soul. This substance is essentially sensory. The *de facto* power
found in this society, therefore, is a mysterious but wholly real
power not existing in created nature, but exercised in it by God
himself directly. In a word, it is an essentially divine power.

740. The *de jure* power has its *title* in this *de facto* power, the
action of God, by which God really communicates himself to
his intelligent creatures and, uniting them to himself in order to
beatify them, creates theocratic society. The society's founder,
the Creator, has the right to administer and govern it because it
was created and founded by him, and because it involves the
fullest submission of the creature to the Creator.

741. The call to such a society, and enrolment in it, is a
supreme, gratuitous benefit from God. Man's refusal to enter
into society with God would be infinite foolishness and impiety.

742. Nevertheless, this society must be voluntary, like every
other. No one adheres to God socially except through willing
assent. God wanted enrolment in the theocratic society to be
similar to that of every other human society. It was to come
about by contract, renewed many times, as we can see, with the
Hebrew people. Christ himself left the decision about following

him to human will, without imposing it upon anyone, 'If anyone will come after me, let him follow me'.

743. On God's part, therefore, enrolment takes place at the
moment of baptism through a divine, deiform action; on the
part of the baptised person, it takes place through express consent and the promise made to adhere to the Church and to her
faith and maxims. By this promise, the Church acquires the
right to unremitting membership from the newly baptised (cf.
USR, 450–451).

744. Those not belonging to the theocratic society remain
subject, with every other creature, to the absolute dominion of
God. But he is only their master, not their fellow-member. For
those not accepting his society, he is a just master, and most holy
vindicator of his justice. Those who attempt to renounce the
perpetual pact they have sworn to him on their entrance to the
society are justly punished as rebel members of the society and
of the lord, its head.

Article 2.
Governmental power in theocratic society is exercised in seven ways

745. The *de facto* power of theocratic society is therefore
infinitely great, and essentially supernatural.

746. At the same time, it is a power *de jure*, in such a way that
God both possesses and exercises it in perfect justice. Hence all
the conditions necessary for the subsistence of a theocratic
society are present; a divine power is present *de facto* and *de
jure*.

747. The divinity exercises this social power in seven ways.

748. The first way consists in the *aggregation* of human creatures to the society, and in the ordained constitution of the
society. As we said, this comes about through the intimate,
hidden action by which God really communicates himself to
souls, giving them some perception of himself. — The three
sacraments of baptism, confirmation and holy orders are ordained for this purpose.

749. The second way consists in the *sacrifice* in which God

died to save the world from sin, offering himself honour equivalent to the greatness of his majesty.

Because he is not subject to death, God took up human nature into a divine person. By giving this human nature of his over to death, he could be said to have died, because his soul was in fact truly divided from his body. This separation of Christ's body and soul must rightly be considered as a sacrifice God made to himself. The person of the Word could say truly, 'No one takes my life from me (it was his very own human life), but I lay it down of my own accord. I have the power to lay it down, and I have power to take it again.'[118] — The sacrament of orders is additionally intended to perpetuate the divine sacrifice.

750. The third way in which God exercises theocratic power consists in the manner by which he *nourishes the members of the society with himself*. He does this by feeding them with the body of his Christ. — The sacrament of the eucharist exists for this purpose.

751. The fourth way consists *in removing the obstacles* to participation in the common good that spring from *the sins* of the members. This is the purpose of the sacraments of penance and extreme unction.

752. The fifth way consists in the grace by which God *disposes the natural society between spouses to the service due to theocratic society*. — The sacrament of matrimony was instituted for this reason.

753. The sixth way consists in an *infallible teaching of supernatural truths*. — This is the purpose of the ministry of the word.

754. Finally, the seventh way consists in the prudential, disciplinary and *external order* amongst members living here on earth. Such order comes from the Spirit of Christ. — This is the purpose of the power of jurisdiction in the episcopate.[119]

755. These seven ways of exercising social power, or seven branches of power in the theocratic society, contain everything necessary for orderly government in its entirety.

The first branch of power is that which constitutes and brings

[118] Jn 10: 18.
[119] 'The Holy Spirit has placed you bishops, TO RULE the Church of God' (Acts 20: 28 [Douai]).

together the society: *its constitutive power*. But because aggregation demands unlimited submission of the creature to the Creator, the second branch is concerned with sacrifice: *liturgical
power*.

The third branch bestows upon members in the fullest manner
the good they are to enjoy as a society of fruition. This enjoyment generates action, that is, the strength to act: *eucharistic
power*.

The fourth branch removes the obstacles preventing members
from obtaining the end of the society: power of purification,
power to bind and loose, healing power.

The fifth branch fuses the natural longings of humanity with
the longing of theocratic society by consecrating to theocratic
society not only the *individual* human being, but the human
species: *hierogenetic power*.

The sixth branch develops the fundamental feeling of God
infused at baptism. This feeling instructs the intellect, freeing it
from error so that human beings can put to work the social good
bestowed upon them at the moment of aggregation: *teaching
power*. — This power has various modes of activity such as
defining the truths to be believed, *interpreting holy Scripture*,
preaching, *teaching*, and so on.

Finally, the seventh branch regulates external means wisely so
that the attainment of the end may not be harmed by outward
disorder. The aim is to help the collective body of members to
reach the social end through the body's perfect organisation:
power of organisation. This power also has various modes of
activity, such as *legislative*, *judicial*, *executive* and *penal* or *sanctioning* power.

Article 3.
Jesus Christ, after exercising governmental power,
communicated it to the Apostles and their successors

756. J ESUS Christ exercised these seven branches of divine
power, and on leaving this world invested his Apostles with the

[756]

sevenfold power, 'As the Father has sent me, even so I send you,'[120] and 'Lo, I am with you always, to the close of the age.'[121]

757. These last words of Christ show that it is he, in his divine person, who carries out theocratic activity while making use of human beings as his ministers and instruments. As the divine person made use of human nature united to himself to carry out divine actions, so the same person makes use of other human persons whom he has really incorporated to himself by uniting them to his divinity and his humanity.

Article 4.
A résumé of the notion of the Church of Jesus Christ. — The earthly hierarchy

758. We are now in a position to sum up what has been said.

1. The Church of Christ is the society of mankind raised to the dignity of perfect theocratic society.

2. This society completes the destiny and the end of mankind, which is to be found in truth, virtue and happiness. The Church has as its own proper end God, where truth, virtue and bliss have their source in his essence, reality and absoluteness.

3. Hence, all human beings are called to the Church, although not all respond to their sublime vocation.

4. The head of the Church is the Word Incarnate, the divine person, who carries out the divine activity proper to theocratic society.

5. Finally, becoming invisible to human eyes, he chose from

---

[120] Jn 20: 21. With these words, Christ gave the Apostles the faculty to send others with the same faculties in the way he himself had been sent, and empowered by the Father to send others.

[121] Mt 28: 20. It may be objected that because baptism can be validly conferred by every human being, Christ did not confer this power upon his Church alone. However, every person who baptises must have the intention of doing what the Church does when she baptises. Otherwise, the baptism is invalid. It is therefore the intention and faith of the Church which is important, and it can be said that a non-believer makes himself an instrument of the Church when he baptises. Cf. *Catechism of the Council of Trent*, p. 2, c. 2: 22, 33.

mankind visible ministers ordered towards unity through the primacy of Peter. These were to be instruments of his divine activity, and constitute the Catholic *hierarchy*.[122]

Article 5.
The fourth mark of the Church — apostolicity

759. A fourth mark, *apostolicity*, has to be added, therefore, to the three already indicated.

760. The first three marks are held in common with the universal society of mankind, although in the Church they are realised, perfected and raised to the supernatural order. The fourth mark is proper to the Church alone.

761. The mark of *apostolicity* shows the Church coming directly from Christ because the Apostles, sent by Christ himself, have been made suitable by him for handing on to future generations his teaching and the supernatural gifts of his Spirit.

This 'note' also distinguishes the true Church from other communions separated from it.[123]

[122] Because I am writing for Catholics, I have no need to prove what they believe. Proofs can be found in books of dogma and apologetics, where they can be consulted if readers wish to do so. My principal aim is to put the ideas together logically, and to offer readers a coherent treatise which itself offers strong proof of the truth for a person who feels that the intrinsic characteristic of truth lies in its perfect, interior harmony.

[123] 'Let [the heretics] show the origins of their churches; let them put forward the order in which their bishops succeeded to one another from the beginning and show that their first bishop had as his maker and predecessor someone from the Apostles, or apostolic men who had persevered with the Apostles. This is how the apostolic churches make up their records. Thus the church at Smyrna has Polycarp, who was placed there by John, and the church of Rome tells us that Clement was ordained by Peter. Let the rest then show those whom they have constituted as bishops to be drawn from the apostolic seed' (Tertullian, d. 215 AD, *De Praescript. haeretic.* c. 32).

Article 6.
The classification of rights in the Church:
connatural and acquired rights

762. Let us now examine briefly the special rights in the theocratic society of the Redeemer. First, let us see how these rights can be classified.

In the first place, we can make use of two classes analogous to those applied to the rights of human individuals which, as we said, are composed of *connatural* and *acquired rights*.

763. Connatural rights in theocratic society are those springing from its nature in such a way that the society, once it begins to exist, is furnished with these rights.

764. Acquired rights in theocratic society are those which it obtains through some legitimate act, but to which it has no title by constitution or essence.

Let us list both kinds of rights briefly.

Article 7.
Connatural rights in the hierarchical Church of the Redeemer

765. Rights connatural to the Redeemer's hierarchical Church, that is, the Catholic Church, regard either all human beings living on earth, or the Church's members only.

§1. *Connatural rights of the Church in its relationship
with all human beings*

766. The Church's connatural rights in its relationship to all human creatures can be reduced to five: the right: 1. to existence; 2. to recognition; 3. to freedom; 4. to propagation; 5. to ownership. Let us say a word about each of these rights.

A.
The right to existence

767. I. *Proofs of this right*:
    1. The Church has the right to exist because it is a lawful

and just society. All lawful and just societies have a natural right to existence.

768. 2. The Church is the society of mankind raised to the supernatural level, and thus realised, is complete. Its only aim is to give human beings full truth, full virtue and full happiness. Now, the society of mankind is of absolute natural right; it is the supreme and essential right of the *human species*, and its object is the end and destiny of the species. Human society cannot and will not renounce this end.[124]

769. 3. The society we are speaking of is superior to all other societies, and is their foundation. It cannot, therefore, be abolished or supplanted by other societies.

770. 4. Voluntary adherence to such a society is also the supreme, essential right of every *human individual*. The exercise of this supreme right cannot be forbidden or blocked by any force or power. Truth, virtue and happiness are connatural and inalienable human rights, the foundation of all other human rights, and consequently the foundation of all possible powers on earth (cf. *RI*, 44–127).

771. 5. The Church of the Redeemer, therefore, is in possession of all these rights even if it is considered simply as identical with the natural society of mankind which it helps, develops, realises and sublimates. It lacks the imperfection and powerlessness present in the natural society of the human race, which points to man's destiny but cannot lead him to it; in fact, it points imperfectly to this destiny because it indicates abstract truth, natural virtue and limited happiness. The theocracy founded by Christ, on the other hand, points man securely to truth, virtue and happiness and bestows them upon him in reality. If, therefore, natural society has an absolute, inalienable right that cannot possess greater force when considered from the natural point of view, such a right, when looked at in Christianity, receives an infinitely greater value and produces an infinitely greater obligation. Right takes its value from the good which produces it,[125] and good in natural society is increased infinitely in Christianity. What was ideal is now real; what was

[124] Cf. *SP*, 219–220.
[125] Cf. *ER*, 252–255.

insufficient is now more than sufficient; what was difficult and impossible to achieve, is now easy and assured.

772. 6. The Catholic Church, therefore, has a connatural, absolute, inalienable, supreme, overwhelming right to exist. It possesses this irrespective of the right received *positively* from God, who founded the Catholic Church. What we have said springs from consideration of its intimate nature viewed in the light of right reason.

773. It may be objected that not everyone recognises the divinity and rights of the Catholic Church, and that not everyone wishes to belong to it.

I reply that the error of some does not destroy the right proper to others. I grant that the person possessing a right must take precautions when exercising it in order not to offend those in the wrong, amongst whom he must be careful to distinguish carefully those erring in good faith from those in bad faith. The former he must treat with the respect we have spoken about elsewhere (cf. *RI*, 457, 1827).

774. Secondly, the error of those not accepting the Church cannot prevent others who believe in the Catholic Church (and I am writing particularly for believers) from recognising the justice and cohesion of my deduction about the Church's connatural right to exist. Catholics cannot support the objection I have just dealt with.

775. Thirdly, the Church's right to free association, held in common with all other naturally lawful societies, requires only the principles of rational Right in order to be recognised. Its lawfulness can only be denied by those wishing to calumniate the Church. But there is no right to calumny. Everyone has to admit the Church's right to exist.

776. Fourthly, persons inside and outside the Church have to recognise facts, and it is an undeniable fact that the Church sets itself no other end than that of helping human beings to reach their natural destiny, which consists in the possession of truth, virtue and happiness. There are only three ways in which objectors can err:

1. By denying that human destiny consists in the possession of these goods; in this case, they err about the elements of rational Right which does not cease to be such because some people ignore or disregard it.

2. By denying that this is in fact the Catholic Church's end; in this case, they show their ignorance of fact, and facts do not change because some people ignore them. Individuals should inform themselves, and recognise the Church's end, purpose and character.

3. By denying that the means used by the Church to reach the end it proposes are suitable for guiding human beings to their destiny; in this case, we have another error of *fact* regarding the divine mission of the Church, its divine power, and so on. People should begin by approving the end the Church sets itself, and then argue about the means by examining the history of its foundation, which presents ample proof of its divine, heavenly origin. This divine origin, and the marvels and other arguments that have persuaded generations for nineteen centuries, and convinced the two hundred million people now believing in the Church, remain what they are. The proofs and truth professed by the whole of the civilised world, by the barbarian world civilised by truth, and the savage world it is civilising now, do not change. Nor is it just or equitable that those knowing the truth should renounce their rights to it or suspend the exercise of these rights until other people have come to know the truth — some will never attain it because they do not want to do so.

777. The Catholic Church and its members would contradict their faith if they did not recognise the Church's *right to existence*, as set out above, and act in accordance with it.

778. II. *The sanction of this right.* — The lawful sanction following from this right is apparent in the character and nature of the right, which we have described previously.

The Church's right to exist forms part of *essential right* (cf. *RI*, 48–52); damage to this right involves *essential injury* (cf. *RI*, 87–127). We have already treated at length the question: 'What kind of force can be used in defence of connatural rights?' (cf. *RI*, 139–238). What we have said can be applied exactly to defence of the right to exist possessed by the society of mankind when raised to the state of Catholic Church.

A few observations need to be added.

The *essential right* of which we are speaking is by nature totally *individual*. Man possesses it as an individual of the human species, whether he is in the natural state with its barely developed personship, or has been raised, as a Christian, to a state of sublimated, developed personship.[126] The faculty for defending such a right *forcefully*, in the manner indicated, is proper to each human being and to each Catholic Christian.

This faculty, therefore, forms part of *communal Right*.

779. Does it not also form part of *governmental Right* in Christian society?

We have seen that government in theocratic society has jural power to teach its members and direct them to their end.

It is the responsibility of Church government, therefore, in so far as it possesses *teaching* and *ordinative power*, to teach and direct the members of the Church in the holiest and most effective exercise of their rights.[127]

Church authority, therefore, can assist its members in the defence of their essential rights[128] by means of *instruction* and *direction*.[129]

B.
The right to recognition

780. Every lawful society has the right to come into being and to exist. In addition, it has the right to recognition (cf. *USR*, 439–445).

The right to recognition means the right according to which all other human beings and societies, without distinction, recognise the bond established within a society by its members; others have to recognise this bond as a *jural fact* giving rise to

---

[126] Cf. We have shown elsewhere that the basis of human personship changes when human beings are placed in the *supernatural order*. Cf. *Dottrina del peccato originale*, q. 5.

[127] Christianity spoke to and cared for *individuals* rather than *societies*. Cf. *SP*, 476–486.

[128] Later in this book, when we analyse the ordinative power of the Church, we shall indicate the special powers of which it is composed.

[129] This teaching could be seen as a way of justifying possible abuse of church authority on the part of persons using it for their own special interests. Such a suspicion would be ill-founded. The teaching does not justify abuses, just as abuses do not destroy the teaching on rights. Cf. *RI*, 459, for the principles followed in developing the most delicate part of the teaching.

rights and obligations. It also means the right according to which all other human beings and societies, in dealing with members of this society, are obliged to respect the rights and obligations which its members have agreed upon amongst themselves, and which constitute their jural state.

781. It follows that recognition of the Church's existence implies recognition of her constitution and of her hierarchic power, together with willingness to treat each of her members in such a way that none of them, in relationship to their fellow-members, is constrained or led to neglect their obligations, or deprived of their socio-theocratic rights.

782. For example, a priest in the United States of America explained that the confessional secret formed part of the constitution and laws of the Catholic Church. As a result, it was felt necessary in that country to release the priest from giving witness in court to what he had heard in confession. In fact, recognition of the Church's jural existence clearly involves corresponding recognition of a Catholic priest's duty towards the secret of confession, and recognition of the socio-theocratic right of the penitent to secrecy about the sins he confesses. If the temporal power had taken a different attitude it would have attempted to constrain the priest to neglect his social obligations, and to deprive the faithful of their social rights. The same argument can be applied proportionately to the purely ministerial secret.

783. The Catholic Church, therefore, has the right to be recognised. The *jural state* of its members, whether simple faithful or rulers holding hierarchical authority, must be recognised by all people and by every society. In a word, recognition is due to the whole complex of their socio-theocratic rights and their obligations.

784. This right springs from the Church's existence as a lawful society, but it is greatly reinforced by the divine marks which confer upon the Church a much firmer right, or rather authority, to exist. These marks have been listed above. The *right to recognition* is the necessary, proximate consequence of the *right to exist*.

C.
The right to freedom

785. The Catholic Church's *right to exist*, and her consequent *right to recognition*, have their source, as we have seen, in the essential right possessed inalienably by every human individual. We have called this right the *right of* absolute *freedom*. By reason of this right, human beings enjoy freedom that can never be justly taken away from them, nor lessened (cf. *RI*, 60–62, 66, 251).

786. In this right to absolute freedom, a distinction can be made between *power* and *virtuality*, that is, between the power of such freedom and the acts virtually contained in the power (cf. *RI*, 82).

The *right to absolute freedom* possessed by every human being refers not only to the power but also to the *virtuality* of absolute freedom.

We have listed several specific actions constituting this virtuality (cf. *RI*, 267), each of which, we said, is the subject of a connatural and inalienable right. One of them is the right of association (cf. *USR*, 432).

787. These rights belong to all individuals as human beings, essentially members of the universal society of mankind.

788. They are also rights possessed by all individuals making up the Church of Jesus Christ.

When individuals enter the Church, their humanity develops and increases, and their personship is enhanced. This is a jural fact, an element in *supernatural Right*. In virtue of this fact, the person, or essential freedom of the human being, requires an infinitely greater respect.

789. The right to freedom, held by all members forming theocratic society, consists in their not being impeded by anyone in the fulfilment of their social obligations and in the exercise of their social rights. Just as these social obligations and rights must be recognised by all (right to recognition), so they must be respected by all in such a way that no obstacle is placed to their fulfilment (right of social freedom). Moreover, there must be no attempt to impede the fulfilment of these rights and duties, unless this occurs indirectly as a result of the exercise by others of their own rights.

[785–789]

790. Freedom in perfect theocratic society, therefore, implies free exercise of all seven powers recognised in it by the members forming the society.

791. Freedom in the same society implies recognition and respect for its suitability and faculty to acquire all rights that can be acquired by naturally lawful, collective bodies in virtue of the natural titles to these rights possessed by all human beings and every other society.

D.
The right to propagation

792. The Catholic Church's right to propagation is established on the following titles:

1. The Catholic Church teaches the truth, and all human beings have the connatural right to communicate the truth to others (cf. *RI*, 147, 267).

793. 2. The Catholic Church is a school of virtue, and all human beings have the connatural right to persuade their fellows to be virtuous (cf. *RI*, 267–269).

794. 3. Membership of the Catholic Church does no harm to anyone; it does good to those joining her. All human beings have the right to do good to others (cf. *RI*, 228–238) (the right to proselytise).

795. 4. The Catholic Church is a lawful society. All lawful societies, having the right to exist, also have the right to invite to membership those wishing to join them.

796. 5. The Catholic Church is the society of mankind elevated to the supernatural level. Hence every human being has the right and the duty to belong to it as soon as he learns about it. The Catholic Church, in working appropriately (cf. *RI*, 269) to draw all to itself, is only helping them to exercise their rights and fulfil their duties. Everyone has the right to offer such beneficial assistance.

797. 6. Finally, the right of propagation comes to the Church from the right of seigniory belonging to God, who has instituted the Church. The right of propagation extends to all human beings and to all societies because God has commanded

the ministers of the Church to preach the gospel to all nations and to baptise them, that is, to enrol them in the theocratic society of Christ.[130]

E.
The right to ownership

798. Finally, the Church has the connatural right to ownership. It is a lawful society, and all lawful societies have this right (cf. 446–449).

We have already seen this, and have moreover shown that no one and no society can limit such a right under the pretext of damage that may ensue from the accumulation of wealth. This damage either does not exist, or can be forestalled, or put right in other genuinely jural ways.

We added, however, that the right to possess ceases in a society when the right is exercised in open contradiction with the end of the society. Can this occur in the case of the Church? We shall discuss this later when we examine the questions of acquired rights in the Church and, in particular, of the property and wealth already acquired by her.

§2. Sanctioning connatural rights in the Church

799. We have spoken elsewhere about the sanction of connatural rights (cf. *RI*, 161–238). We have also mentioned sanction related to the Church's right to existence (cf. 778–779). The reader may refer to what we have said.

§3. The rights of all human beings relative to the Church

800. The Church's rights relative to all human beings and all societies, which we have mentioned above, call forth corresponding

[130] Mt 28: 18–20; Mk 16: 15.

rights towards the Church in all individuals and societies. These rights are as follows.

A. *The right to know the Church*. People could not be obliged to recognise the Catholic Church if they did not first know her for what she is. — The right to know the Church is connatural in all, just as their right to know the truth is connatural. The exercise of this right is linked with their duty to acknowledge the Church, which they are obliged to acknowledge practically only in so far as they know her. If they know her as a lawful society, that is, free from immorality but nothing more, their obligation to acknowledge her is not as great as it would be if they knew her as a society founded by God himself for the salvation and perfection of mankind. — The *right to know* brings with it the *right to examine*, but it does not authorise wrongful or biased examination, nor illogical method in correct examination, nor any other abuse in the employment of such a right.

801. B. *The right to join*. Because the Church is the society of mankind raised to a sublime level, every human being, precisely because he is human, has the right to be accepted for membership in the Church when he believes in the gospel he has received. This right is conditioned, however, by the individual's willingness to submit to the social conditions required of persons joining the society.

802. C. *The right to protection*. — Every human being and every society has the right to protect the rights of others, but especially the rights of the Church. This is a beneficent and religious act (cf. *USR*, 167–168). It does not mean, however, that anyone possesses a *right of wardship* over the Church. Such a right involves superiority, and no individual or society is superior to the Church.

803. We also need to note that the right to protect the Church does not justify interference in her internal affairs. This applies even more strongly to the use of force against the Church's rulers in order to impede their freedom of government. Nor does the use of this right allow the usurpation of other rights. The abuse of the right to protection is not to be confused with the exercise of such a right.

§4. *The Church's connatural rights relative to its members*

A.
Rights

804. Relative to its members, the Church has the right to exercise freely the seven powers we have listed. All the members have the jural duty to submit to the sevenfold power, which they have acknowledged by their entrance to the Church.

805. Every ordinary member of the Church depends upon her government, as the member of any society depends upon its government. We have already stated the principles according to which this dependence is determined. The most important is consideration of the requirements of the society's constitution.

806. Here it is sufficient to note that *directive power* (cf. 779) in the Church is intended to regulate the life of the faithful and the exercise of their rights by aiding, not impeding their sanctification. Consequently, such power is very extensive, and has a lawful, although indirect and moral, influence, even over temporal matters.

We offer some brief observations about the sanction governing these rights in the Church.

B.
Sanctions

807. To which power does the Church's right of sanction over her members belong?

Sanctions can be considered as a *function proper to every right*.[131] From this point of view, each of the seven powers provides its own sanction. The sanction of *constitutive power*, for example, is a function of this power, and so on for the other powers.

808. In the second place, the right of sanction can be considered as a *force or effective power* (the 'matter' of right). From

---

[131] Cf. *ER*, 246–251.

this point of view, the power of sanction is the result of linking several powers, amongst which are the power of binding and loosing, of imposing penances, of depriving the faithful of ecclesiastical benefits, and so on.

809. Finally, the right of sanction can be considered as an *executive means*. From this point of view, it belongs to *directive power*, which includes executive power, and becomes one of its functions.

810. What kind of sanction does the Church use to strengthen the exercise of its powers relative to its members?

We have seen that the Church's rights relative to all human beings can be defended against aggressors even by external force, provided it is employed correctly. As we said, anyone may help the Church in this way (cf. *RI*, 144–238). This is not the case with the Church's rights relative to her members, that is, with the rights that church government possesses relative to its subjects. Sanctions of these rights are essentially pacific.[132]

811. What gives rise to the difference between the sanction of the Church's rights relative to all human beings, and that of the rights of church government relative to the members of the Church?

The rights of the Church relative to all human beings are those which bring her into existence and maintain her power to act. Defence of these rights is defence of her existence and her activity. External force can help to prevent the Church's overthrow in a country, and can therefore be used by anyone against others who abuse force by attacking the Church or her freedom to act (cf. *RI*, 203–207).

812. On the other hand, all the rights of church government towards her members tend solely to the sanctification of the

[132] It should be noticed that the Church's rights relative to all mankind are rights she necessarily possesses over her own members in whose regard she can uphold these rights forcefully just as she does with human beings in general. The Church can also defend her *acquired rights* with force against her own members, as we shall see later. For example, when Theodosius removed the Arian bishop, Demophilus, from the see of Constantinople (380 AD), he defended: 1. the Catholic Church's *connatural right* to exist (Arianism, which was not the Church, was killing the Church); 2. *rights acquired* over church buildings and other ecclesiastical possessions at Constantinople, usurped violently and unjustly by the heretics.

members which is not brought about by force. An individual is good and holy only in so far as he clings to justice and charity through his own interior, spontaneous act. Force would be useless for such a purpose because it could not conserve the sole good sought by the Church in the exercise of her rights, nor could it maintain the rights of which we are speaking. Right deprived of its good is no right at all.[133]

813. We must also note that the external force which sanctions the Church's rights relative to all human beings, is not to be used, properly speaking, by church government, but by the members of the Church. Ecclesiastical government itself has a pacific mission, the sanctification of the members of the Church.

The right of sanction relative to the Church's right to exist and operate freely is a right inherent in every individual as such. Its origin is not to be found, strictly speaking, in church government, which can only direct human beings in the best and holiest exercise of their rights. It cannot give them the rights themselves, nor exercise them in their place.

814. What sanction can church government use to maintain the rights it exercises relative to the members of the society it rules?

The sanction consists in two powers:

1. the power to impose penance, and

2. the power to deprive the unrepentant of the benefits they possess in the Church.

815. The *power to impose penance* extends to inflicting corporal and temporal punishment of all kinds (*the first type of punishment*), except capital punishment and punishments which of their nature slowly destroy life. These lawful punishments, although corporal and temporal, do not in fact come under the heading of sanction by force, because this is imposed with violence. Penances imposed by the Church are always accepted voluntarily by the faithful on whom they are imposed. Faith alone, not external force, is the stimulus prompting the members to accept the penance, because they believe their eternal salvation depends upon reconciliation with God and the

---

[133] 'Some good present in the action', is the third constitutive element of right. Cf. *ER*, 252–255.

Church. Penance is imposed as a condition of their reconciliation. Here, the Church although lawfully exercising power over temporal things, does not impose it violently. It is accepted willingly by the members, as their duty demands.[134]

816. *The power to exclude the unrepentant from sharing in the benefits of the Church (the second type of punishment)* consists principally in refusing them absolution from sin. This is a spiritual sanction, nothing more, and is carried out fully when exercised by the Church through excommunication.

817. Although this power is entirely spiritual, it has certain necessary temporal consequences, as we shall see immediately.

First, participation in church benefits requires external acts. Those deprived of these benefits are excluded from the external, material acts by which they are benefited. Refusal of these benefits itself entails external, material acts.

Second, the Church sometimes excludes the unrepentant from external acts common to the body of the faithful for two reasons: to help them realise the horror of the fault committed; and to safeguard the rest of the faithful from infection. Regret and punishment, which must result as the guilty see themselves cut off externally from other members, is a kind of *penance* and, in so far as the separation is something they have to accept for themselves, an *obligatory command* that can be carried out only spontaneously and willingly. In so far as the rest of the faithful are obliged to have nothing to do with excommunicated persons, such ecclesiastical punishment can be considered globally as a penance inflicted on the persons excommunicated, as a public profession of faith by those avoiding them and thus manifesting their disagreement with them, and finally as a precaution against the spread of the contagion amongst the faithful in general.

818. *A third kind of punishment* may be inflicted as a mode of forceful sanction of the Church's laws. In this case, sanctions are employed to overcome material obstacles to obedience to the laws; force helps persuasion by correcting recalcitrant animal instinct, and is useful in dealing with children, with the insane,

---

[134] Public penances go back to the first centuries of the Church's history. Cf. Tertullian, *Apol.*, c. 39; *De Pud.*, c. 5; *De Poen.*, c. 9; St. Irenaeus, *Contra Haer.*, bk. 1, c. 13, nn. 5–6.

and with uncouth people, as I have noted elsewhere.[135] Great wisdom is needed, however, in applying this force, which is more of a stimulus than a sanction. Its use should be moderated according to the grossness of the persons concerned, and abandoned as soon as it is clear that opposition to church law arises from lack of instruction or from badly disposed will, rather than from material instinct.

819. Nevertheless, this kind of force also is never inflicted directly by church government, although it can be employed by a Christian people, by a father towards his children, by superiors towards their subjects, and so on.

820. This kind of force, and the other sanctions we have spoken of, are not to be confused with punishments inflicted by temporal government upon heretics or others whose offences against the laws of the Church are considered harmful to the State. This is a *fourth class of punishment* aimed at eliminating failings against the rights of the Church.

821. Punishments of this nature have a place provided they are aimed at truly criminal offences, such as riots and rebellion, disturbance of individuals' civil liberties, violence, killings and so on. Such crimes deserve punishment, irrespective of their cause, although the cause may justly provoke severer punishment necessary to suppress the criminal impulse producing the cause.[136]

822. Finally, we should note that these last two classes of punishment have sometimes coincided. When civil government wished to suppress disorders in civil society arising from rebellion against the Church, and the Church wished to chastise her children in order to lead them to penance, church and civil

---

[135] Cf. *AMS*, 735–737. The Scriptures speak of this kind of paternal punishment as useful and just. Cf. Prov 13: 23; Sir 30: [1–2].

[136] Heresies have always been the cause of public unrest. This is one of the principal reasons why governments decreed the use of temporal punishment against heretics (*Cod. Theod.*, 1. *Just.* 1:1, *De Fide Catholica; C. Th.*, 14: 4, *De his qui super religione contendunt; Cod. Th.*, 16: 5, *Just.* 1: 5, *De haereticis*). In the 13th century, rebellion and violence compelled rulers to issue new, severe laws against heretics. Cf., for example, those decreed by St. Louis of France (1228 AD), and those of Frederick II (1234 AD). Spanish royal edicts are known only too well. In Russia, even in the last century, heresies originating in the Russian church were punished with burning.

authority agreed in inflicting certain punishments on offenders.[137]

Article 8.
The Church's acquired rights

§1. *The source of acquired rights in the Church*

823. As we have seen (cf. *RI*, 284), the right to *innate, relative freedom* is the source of acquired rights.

Such freedom is proper to isolated individuals, and to individuals in association, that is, societies (cf. *USR*, 426–449). It is a complex right, embracing the right to every kind of ownership.

824. Generally speaking, every society possesses this connatural right to acquire all kinds of ownership and material dominion, provided it does so under just titles common to all mankind (cf. *USR*, 446–449).

---

[137] Examples of such mixed punishments are, I think, those sometimes inflicted by the Church herself with the support of civil authority.

For instance:

1. *Exile*, mentioned in the Roman Council (503 AD) under Symmachus; Constantinople III, *Act.* 7; Orleans IV, can. 29; Toledo XII, can. 10: S. Gregory the Great, bk. 2, ep. 71. *ad Arthemium*, and the *Codex of Canon Law*, can. 3, distinct. 3; can. , c. 3; quaest. 4; can. 3.

2. *Floggings*, mentioned in St. Augustine (*Ep.* 133, bk. 2 *ad Marcellinum Trib.*); St. Cyprian (5., Surio in the *Vita di S. Cesario*, 24th August.); St. Gregory the Great (bk. 4. *Ep.* 27; bk. 5, *Ep.* 65); Cassian (*Instit.* bk. 4, c. 16); Palladius (*Hist. Lausic.* c. 7); the Councils of Agde (can. 38, 41, *ap.* Labb. t. 5, col. 527–528); of Narbonne, under Recardeus (can. 13, *ap.* Labb. t. VI, col. 728); Epaon (can. 13, *ap.* Labb. t. 5, col. 713); and of Mâcon (can. 8, *ap.* Labb. 6, col. 660).

3. *Fines*, mentioned in Coun. of Carthage V, c. 400 AD (*ap.* Labb. t. II, col. 1454), in St. Augustine (*Ep.* 104), and St. Gregory the Great (bk. 4, *Ep.* 26).

4. Ecclesiastical *imprisonment*, mentioned by the Emperors Arcadius and Honorius (Leg. 30. *Cod. Theod. de Haeret.*); by Justinian (*Nov.* 79, cap. 2); by the *Capitularies* of Charlemagne (bk. 5, *ap.* Balut.); by Basil the Deacon (*Libell. ad Teod. et Valentinian. in actis Concilii Ephes.*, P. 1, c.30); by Gregory II (*Ep. ad. Leon. Isaar. ap.* Labb t. 8, col. 671); by the Councils of Mâcon (*ap.* Labb. t. 6, col. 65); of Seville (*ivi* col. 1314), and of Epaon (*ivi* t. 5, col. 711).

In applying this principle to the Church, we concluded that she was as free as other individuals and societies to acquire rights and ownership of any kind without limit, granted just title.[138]

§2. *The acquired rights of the Church*

825. The various jurisdictions and acquired rights of the Church are dominion and ownership accruing to her by just title, and every other right which is not a necessary consequence of her constitution and of divine right.

An objection is possible at this point. As we said, a society's end sets limits to its social right to ownership: societies can own only if, and in so far as, their possessions are not excluded by their end, or are not harmful to that end. But the end of the Church is totally spiritual; it has been founded only for the sanctification of mankind. It would seem, therefore, that temporal rights of ownership and dominion are excluded from the Church's end.

826. This objection merits careful attention. From the time of Julian the Apostate, it has often been repeated, and on occasion has prevailed as solid right.

A society's end can be related to temporal goods in three ways:

1. It can *require them* if their acquisition constitutes the end of the society, or if they are indispensable means to the attainment of its end.

---

[138] Although the Christian religion was not *positively* recognised by the government under the pagan emperors, no one doubted that it had the same right to possess as all other societies. Roman legislation implicitly recognised the right to possess in all societies not expressly prohibited by law or by the supreme power. Hence Christians could appeal to Aurelian when Paul of Samosata, excommunicated by the Council of Antioch, refused to leave the bishop's residence. The emperor decided (271 AD) that the decision about ownership of the house should be left to the Italian bishops, and in particular to the decision of the bishop of Rome (*Eusebius, Histor.*, bk. 7, c. 23). Licinius' edict (313 AD) illustrates the same point. It does not authorise the Church to possess, but requires restitution of the temporalities of which she had been robbed. This shows that there was no argument about her natural right to possess, which was taken for granted. We have quoted elsewhere the relevant words of the edict.

2. It is able *not to reject them* although they may not be absolutely necessary to the society's end.

3. Finally, it may *exclude them* and totally reject them.

827. Only in the last case, as we said, is any society constitutionally incapable of ownership. Amongst such societies are those religious orders whose members have vowed publicly to renounce any kind of civil possession. This is not the case, however, with church society in general whose end, therefore, does not exclude its faculty to acquire temporal rights, and to possess.[139]

§3. Two classes of church temporalities: those needed for clergy maintenance, proper to the clergy; those dedicated to pious works for the benefit of communities of the faithful, proper to the community

828. What is the relationship between the Church's end and temporal goods and rights?

The word 'Church' is sometimes taken to mean the government of the Church, the *clergy*, the complex of its ministers.

---

[139] The best judge of what is required for a society's end is the society itself, because its end is as important to it as its existence. This principle is applicable in a special way to the Church, which is always assisted by her divine Founder. The Church has never doubted her faculty for possessing, as we can see in the references given in Mammachi who amply refers to and defends the Church's feelings in the matter. Here, I shall simply refer to certain councils which take for granted this right of the Church to acquire rights and temporalities. Ecumenical councils: Chalcedon (451 AD), Act. 6, can. 2; Act. 10, can. 26. — Lateran I (1123 AD), can. 1. — Lateran II (1139 AD), can. 25. — Lateran III (1179 AD), can. 15, 19. — Lateran IV (1215 AD), can. 46. — Lyons II gen. (1274 AD), can. 12, 22. — Constance (1414 AD), sess. 8. — Trent, sess. 22, c. 11. Other Councils suppose or declare the same right of the Church, amongst them the following: Ancyra (314 AD), can. 15. — Antioch (341 AD), can. 24. — Constantinople (536 AD). — Trullo (7th cent. AD), can. 35. — Mainz (428 AD). — Paris III (767 AD), can. 1. — Paris V (1050 AD), can. 9. — Paris VI (1105 AD), can. 15. — Arles (452 AD), can. 47. — Mâcon (581 AD), can. 4. — Lyons II partic. (567 AD), can. 2. — Tours (566 AD), can. 24, 25. — Orleans I (511 AD). — Orleans II (533 AD). — Orleans III (538 AD). — Orleans IV (645 AD). — Orleans V (1017 AD), cap. 13 *ss.* — Trier I (895 AD), cap. 7.

Sometimes it stands for the *community of all the faithful*. Let us examine the relationship between the clergy's end and temporalities, and that between the end of the community of the faithful and their temporal goods.

829. First, the clergy's end requires some temporal goods as a condition of their subsistence. The clergy's right to depend for subsistence upon stipends for time dedicated to the exercise of the ministry, and therefore no longer available for earning a living or decently enriching oneself, is assured by rational, theocratic Right, and by divine, positive right.[140]

830. The clergy, therefore, have in common with all men and women, and with all societies, the right to acquire temporal goods on the basis of just titles. In addition, they have their own proper title, in their quality as church ministers, to require their necessary sustenance from the community of the faithful to whom they minister spiritual things. The faithful are jurally obliged to provide what is necessary for the purpose.

831. What is the relationship between the end for which the clergy exist and the temporal goods superfluous to their maintenance? Are these required necessarily by their end, or excluded and rejected by the end? — Neither one nor the other. The end for which the clergy exist does not absolutely require these goods, nor does it exclude or reject them. The only condition to be observed relative to this end is that the clergy use goods superfluous to their maintenance for pious purposes. In this way, such temporalities are not an impediment, but an aid

[140] Mt 10: 9–15; Mk 6: 8–11; Lk 9: 3–5; 10: 4–12. In these pages, JESUS Christ frees his ministers from preoccupation about necessary temporalities by obliging the faithful whom they serve to provide food, housing and everything else needed by their pastors. 'Christ shows clearly why he did not wish them to possess and be burdened with these things. It was not that they were not necessary for sustaining life, but because he sent the Apostles in such a way as to show that they were owed these things, the soldiers' pay, as it were, by those believers to whom they would announce the Gospel' (St. Augustine, *De Consensu Evangel.* bk. 2, c. 30). JESUS Christ commands the faithful under grave penalty to provide what is necessary; he leaves further contributions to the generosity of the faithful. He wants his ministers to be content with what is necessary without refusing the spontaneous, additional offerings the faithful may care to make. 'And remain in the same house, eating and drinking what they provide, for the labourer deserves his wages.' Cf. also 1 Cor 9: 1–15, and St. John Chrysostom, *Hom.* 66 in Mt 5.

to the sanctification of the faithful, the end for which Christ instituted the clergy.

832. Having distinguished what is necessary for the clergy's maintenance in their special work from what is superfluous to such maintenance, we have to conclude:

1. That the clergy have a special, proper title to maintenance which obliges the Christian community to provide for them.

2. That while the clergy have no special, proper title to what is superfluous to their maintenance, no one is free to deprive the clergy of the jural freedom by which they acquire such goods in accord with just titles common to all individuals and to all lawful societies. Moreover, the clergy cannot be deprived of the freedom to administer and dispose the temporalities they have acquired, although they are obliged to use them for pious causes, that is, in encouraging piety and in exercising charity.

833. It is true that temporal charity, which can be exercised by all the faithful, is not work exclusive to the clergy. Hence, when the clergy feed the hungry, clothe the naked, care for the sick, and carry out other works of corporal charity, they do not, strictly speaking, act as clergy.

And this shows even more clearly that the clergy have the right to use in pious works the temporalities they have acquired by just title, or hold as trustees or administrators. Members of the clergy do not cease to be members of the Church, nor do they lose the rights inherent to their position as simple faithful. The greater contains the less.

§4. *It is natural, useful and fitting for the clergy to administer the goods owned by the community of the faithful and designated for pious works which benefit the community*

834. Each of the faithful can exercise temporal charity on his own, or through others.

835. If the Christian people, of whom the clergy are a part, entrusts to the clergy temporalities which it consecrates to works of charity and religion, it does not exceed its rights. Nor do the clergy overstep their right in accepting administration

and distribution of these goods. It is natural, useful and fitting that matters should be arranged in this way.

836. It is *natural*, because to trust its teachers, its shepherds and spiritual fathers is natural to people who see that certain persons have been set aside from earthly things for the sake of divine service, and have undertaken to live as models of virtue.

837. It is *useful*, because the clergy offer the people the best possible guarantee of faithful and enlightened administration, granted their knowledge and virtue, and granted the special circumstances which enable them to recognise and provide for real human necessity in the most suitable way. In fact, delicacy is often needed to avoid embarrassing indigent people; impartiality and economy are required in the distribution and administration of goods; finally (this is supremely important), there is the problem of spiritual assistance for those being helped materially. All this can best be faced by the clergy.

838. We should recognise that material help can be of great assistance in the sanctification of the faithful, which is the special work of priests. When material help is employed for this purpose, it not only alleviates misery, but eliminates its causes.

839. Finally, it is *fitting* because it is becoming that through such works, which generate greater respect and affection for those to whom they are entrusted, the clergy's most holy work of ministry should be facilitated. In any case, the clergy have the right to intervene in administration to ensure that the will of the donors is not frustrated.[141]

840. Churchmen, therefore, administer and distribute goods set aside for pious works, but they do this, as far as strict right is concerned, as simple members of the faithful designated for the purpose by their fellow-members. But it is especially fitting that they should be designated for this work.

---

[141] The Council of Trent permits donors to nominate lay people, as well as clergy, as administrators of pious foundations. Benefactors may also decide who are to receive the accounts submitted by the administration, although it is understood that provision should be made for the inclusion amongst these persons of the Ordinary of the diocese, 'unless indeed this has been expressly catered for in the establishment and ordinance of such a church or building' (Sess. 32, *De Reform*. c. 9).

§5. *The temporalities destined by Catholics for pious use are different from national goods*

841. At this point, we can examine the Church's right to ownership relative to her existence as a fellowship of the faithful, not simply as clergy.

842. The fellowship of the faithful, amongst whom the clergy are certainly included, is a society capable of common, unlimited ownership, on the basis of just titles.

843. The title to ownership is normally that which also determines the use of the goods.

844. I say 'normally' because it is certain that Christian fellowship would act within its rights if it were to accumulate goods without any attempt to determine their use, leaving this to the free decision of the fellowship itself. In this case, however, such temporalities could not be called 'church goods' because they would not have been devoted to pious or charitable uses. The *faithful* would have simply acted as *human beings*. They do not cease to be such because they are faithful, just as *churchmen* do not cease to be members of the *faithful*.

845. But if the goods which they have put together are dedicated expressly or implicitly to charity or religion, this end must be maintained. If a person has left money or property for the construction of a church or hospital on a given site, the local community of the faithful is indeed the owner of these goods. Its ownership, however, is restricted and conditioned by the object for which the goods were donated or willed. The community of the faithful cannot use them for a purpose other than that established by the will of the donor.

846. If the donor's will cannot be carried out, his disposition, according to simple rational Right, becomes null.

847. Ownership lasts and is transmitted as long as the community for which it is given remains in existence.

848. If the administration of gifts has not been established by will of the donor, the community for whose use they have been donated and which has become their owner, can choose the administrator it thinks most suitable. In the case of a Catholic community, however, equity, utility, fittingness and church law naturally require bishops and lower churchmen to undertake the major part of this duty.

849. On the other hand, justice demands that goods be applied solely to the objects determined by the express or presumed will of the person donating them. People using them for other purposes lose their *just title* and become thieves.

850. Temporalities of this kind do not belong to the nation, or municipalities, but to the *community of the faithful*, to the Church. The nation, or municipalities, may belong to a different religion from that destined for the pious legacy, or it may embrace people of various religious communities. The Church, I have to insist, is different from the nation, dioceses are different from civil provinces, and parishes from municipalities. The two societies, civil and ecclesial, cannot be confused. As jural persons, they are distinct from one another.[142]

851. It is clear from what we have said that the proposal of the unwary bishop of Autun, and the consequent decree of the national assembly declaring church goods in France to be temporalities belonging to the nation,[143] denied all competence to jural titles. The decree was carried out by brute force, and entailed as many thefts as there were testators and donors who had willed to the Church goods destined for religious or beneficent purposes.[144] This was not the first, and it will not be the last, but it is certainly the greatest usurpation achieved until the present.

[142] This confusion of ideas still prevails in French law. Churches and restored presbyteries were declared town properties in the *Avis du Conseil d'État du 2 pluviose XIII* (22nd January, 1805).

[143] Decree of 24th November, 1789 (13 *brumaire* II). Ecclesiastical temporalities of the German provinces on the left bank of the Rhine were also declared national property by the Consuls by decree of 9th June, 1802 (20 *prairial* X).

[144] Sièyes' speech on this occasion (10th August, 1789), printed under the title *Observations sommaires sur les biens ecclésiastiques*, merits attention. 'Although the nation is the supreme legislator (it must be remembered that this was the period of revolutionary *absolutism*), it cannot deprive me of my property nor of my opinion. The principles of all legislation contain guarantees for ownership. How can the legislator deprive me of my ownership if his only reason for existence is to protect it?' Again: 'Ecclesiastical temporalities, like all others, belong to those specifically named as owners by the donors who, although they were free to use them in any legitimate way, have in fact and under the disposition of the law BEQUEATHED THEM TO THE CLERGY AND NOT TO THE NATION.'

852. Lately, revolutionary, anarchical and totalitarian principles of public utility and reasons of State have lost some of the power they exercised over men's minds. Already room is being made for the eternal dictates of rational Right as sources of peace and order. It has been recognised in many places that church goods, that is, those destined for worship or for charity, are essentially different from national goods, and can never be confused with them. Various constitutions have explicitly declared 'that such goods can never be incorporated into the State demesne'.[145]

§6. *Sanctioning the acquired rights of the Church*

853. The Church's acquired rights would be stable and suffer no violation if RIGHT itself were fully and universally known, and had received from states and nations the respect it deserves. Yet because it still needs to be understood that RIGHT alone provides an unshakeable guarantee of peace and prosperity, it is not a waste of time to consider the possibility of some sanction for maintaining the rights acquired by the Church, and ask if it differs from the two kinds of sanction proper to connatural rights.

854. It differs in the sense that the rights of the Church can be divided into three classes according to the quality of their sanctions. The three classes are made up of: 1. connatural rights relative to every human being; 2. connatural rights proper to the Church's own members; 3. acquired rights. The sanction proper to the first group of connatural rights is *force*; to the second

---

[145] The *Constitutions* of Poland, 27th Nov. 1815, §13 — of Baveria, 26th May 1818, tit. 4, §9, 10; *Edict of Religion* of Baveria, 26th May 1818, §3l, 44–49 — The *Constitutions* of Baden, 22nd August 1818, §20 — of Würtemberg, 25th Sept. 1819, §77, 82 — of the Grand Duchy of Hessen, 17th December 1820, §43, 44 — of Saxony — Saxe-Coburg 8th August 1821, §29, 30 — of Saxony — Saxe-Meiningen, 23rd August 1829, art. 33 — of the Electorate of Hessen, 5th January 1831, §138 — of Altenburg, 29 April 1831, §155 — of the kingdom of Saxony, 4th September 1831, §60 — of Hanover, 26th September 1833, §68.

group, *spiritual penalties*; to the third, whatever defends and maintains the rights of nature itself (ownership and dominion) for all other human beings.

855. Owners and those possessing material dominion find in the force proper to civil society the means required to help them protect what they have against injustice and rapacity. For the same reason, the fellowship of the faithful and the Church can make use of the courts to have their rights upheld.

856. It is certain that if civil courts did not exist, or did not enforce proper justice, natural sanctions would be available to the Church as they would be for any other proprietor. (cf. *RI*, 146–151).

857. If we consider the matter historically and factually, we can see that civil authority has never given the same degree of protection to church temporalities and rights as it has to lay temporalities. Very often those in charge of government have taken control of those goods and rights in the name of civil authority. As a result, the Church, the clergy and the communities of the faithful to which the clergy belong have stood before civil society and its government in the same jural relationship as that possessed by one person towards another in the state of nature.

858. This is an undeniable historical fact. The principal violations of acquired rights, and despoliations of ownership suffered by the Church from people invested with civil authority, and often acting in the name of that authority, are briefly described in a modern German work:

> From the time of the Merovingians, laymen had extorted from the king enfeoffment of church goods through special pleading and powerful patronage. Charles Martel[146] and Charlemagne[147] had made use of it in times of crisis to

---

[146] *Chron. Virdun.* (Bouquet t. 3. p. 364): '(Charles) dared to take away the ecclesiastical lands and hand them over to his comrades-in-arms. In the end, he was not afraid to give even bishoprics to lay people.'

[147] *Capit. Caroli M.* (743 AD), c. 2. Benedict. Levit. *Capit.* bk. 5, c. 6; bk. 6, c. 175. A compromise had to be reached with the king, to whom the Church ceded part of her possessions. The king granted them to those fighting for him, and paid a small recognition to the Church. At the death of the final beneficiary, however, such possessions had to be returned to the Church unless the king had obtained from the Church the faculty of granting them

pay off their armies. Charlemagne did in fact promise
sincerely, on his own behalf and that of his descendants, to
abstain from disposing of church temporalities without the
consent of the bishops.[148] But after the reign of Charles the
Bald, who made use of such concessions,[149] many churches
and monasteries remained in the hands of laymen[150] who
not only had the usufruct of the lands, but also retained the
tithes and other income;[151] they granted churchmen only
sufficient for their maintenance. — Another circumstance
favouring lay appropriation of church income may be
found in the conversion into parishes of private chapels of
estate owners. The owners, as founders of the parishes,
claimed the tithes for themselves despite the prohibitions
of church law.[152] Later on, the popes tried to reclaim tithes
for their original beneficiaries, and remove them from the
sphere of commerce to that of the spirit.[153] Many were
retained by laymen, however, who used them in the same
way as their other goods. In 1179 the third Lateran Council[154] again obliged laymen to restitution, and forbade further alienations. Effects of the ruling varied. Some tithes
were renounced, but in favour of monasteries and pious
foundations rather than the churches from which they
were originally taken. The popes themselves eventually
gave their consent to this, provided the local bishop

once more to others.

[148] *Capit. Acquisgran.* 816 (817 AD) c. 1. — *Capit. Reg. Francor.* bk. 1, C.
77; bk. 6, c. 427; bk. 7, c. 142, 261.

[149] This is shown in the concordat agreed with the bishops of the Council
held at Beauvais (845 AD), c. 3: 5.

[150] *Edict. Caroli II de tributo Nordmannico* (877 AD): *De ecclesiis vero,
quas comites et vasalli dominici habent, etc.* — Regino, *De eccles. discipl.* bk.
1, c. 10: *Ut (episcopi) ecclesias tam a regibus in beneficium datas, quam et
aliorum, summo studio provideant.*

[151] Agobard. (d. cir. 840 AD), *De dispens. rerum eccles.* c. 15. 'At this time,
they have acted against the pious wishes of our predecessors by thinking that
it is lawful to sell not only the fabric of the churches, which they have
succeeded in vindicating for themselves, but those things which many of the
faithful have devoutly set aside for their own burial or other holy purposes.'

[152] Council of Coblenz (922 AD), c. 5. 'If lay people have their own chapels,
it is irrational and contrary to authority for them to take tithes and use them
for feeding their dogs and their concubines.'

[153] C. 17: 10, *De decim.* (3, 30); c. 7: 10, *De praescript.* (2. 26); c. 9: 10, *De
rerum permut.* (3, 19).

[154] C. 14.

agreed.[155] The majority of laymen completely refused to make restitution,[156] and the decree of the Council gradually received a broader interpretation: ancient enfeoffed tithes could remain in lay hands provided that their possessors ceased alienating them for themselves, and received no further concessions of tithes. But this interpretation was soon a dead letter. Tithes which had previously fallen into the hands of lay-people were treated in the same way as the rest of their property, and subjected to every type of alienation. They took on the nature of sources of income acquired through civil right of tithes alone. Only here and there was the custom retained of investing the Church with them.[157]

Later, in the 16th century, we find the Church suffering enforced despoliation of her goods. In Russia, Catherine II (1746 AD) took her turn in grabbing church property, which she first placed under the administration of an 'economic committee', and finally within the sphere of State ownership. The clergy were then given salaries. Catherine's policy has recently been repeated by the reigning Czar against the temporalities of the Catholic Church in Poland.[158] We know only too well what happened to church goods in France at the time of the revolution.[159] In Germany, church lands and episcopal domains, along with goods belonging to chapters, abbeys and monasteries, were secularised to indemnify secular princes, although goods used for worship and charitable foundations were respected.[160] In Sweden, church goods were severely attacked; two-thirds of abbatial tithes were confiscated by the crown (1528). In Denmark, church goods were divided equally between the throne, the Church and the pastor. Revolutionary

---

[155] C. 7: 10, *De his quae fiunt a praelatis* (3: 10); c. 3: 10, *De privileg.* (5, 33); c. 2, §3, *De decim. in VI* (3: 13).

[156] This is shown by the Diet of Gelnhausen (1186 AD) in which Urban III put pressure on Frederick I to propose the idea.

[157] Cf. M. Ferd. Walter in his outstanding *Manual of Ecclesiastical Law* (8th ed. 1839), bk. 6, c. l, §243–244.

[158] Ukase of 6th January, 1842, imposed on the sacred Synod, and the executive Senate. The Pope and the Polish clergy protested.

[159] Tithes in France were expropriated without any indemnity. Cf. *Décret des 4–11 août*, 1789, art. 5.

[160] *Rapport de la députation de l'empire du 25 fév.* §34–37, 61, 63, 65.

Spain imitated France by declaring church temporalities to be 'goods belonging *to the nation*'. In Switzerland flagrant attempts to confiscate church goods are being made at the present moment. The combination of an apposite Article (12) in the federal agreement, of the influence of the great powers of Europe and of the threat of civil war were not sufficient to guarantee the defence and maintenance of goods belonging to a few poor monasteries of the tiny canton of Aargau.

859. Notorious, constant and repeated facts of this kind show clearly that the rights and temporalities of the Church have never been sufficiently defended by civil laws ensuring private ownership. Such laws deserve scrutiny by decent, religious, Christian legislators.

860. What are the possible causes of the great diversity between security granted by civil authority to the rights and property of private individuals, and the lack of protection afforded to church rights and goods? There are two principal causes, and they merit careful consideration.

1. The imperfect state of the science of Right. As long as this science has not been firmly established and universally determined, it gives rise to false ideas about the power of civil authority. Such theories sometimes play down the powers of civil authority, and sometimes exaggerate them; they may spring from people hostile or obsequious to the State, or from others who wish to cover unjust actions with a cloak of decency favourable to their own interest. As long as the science of Right is uncertain and obscure, each section chooses without hesitation the teachings that confirm its own advantage, and maintains that its actions are justified by one or other of the controverted theories of Right. The voice of conscience is more easily suppressed if the chosen theory favours the extension of civil authority, because anything supporting civil authority is seen as respectable and sacred. Theories of this kind are highly suitable for easing the consciences of people who recognise their advantage. High-ranking persons always see them as more favourable than the other theories (although in reality this is not the case) and thus have no difficulty in seconding them. The Church has been legally despoiled of her rights on innumerable occasions by such theories and will have to wait until sufficient progress has been made in the study of rational Right in order to enjoy

the solid guarantees she needs. Meanwhile, she must continue her work of establishing the true, impartial principles of Right in men's minds. The best parts of modern legislation do in fact depend upon what the Church has given to the world.

861. 2. The imbalance between church ownership and civil power in which the Church shares. — This is a reason founded in the science of political equilibrium, with which I shall deal in the fourth book on social right. *De facto* civil power is only an aggregate of the powers of all the members of civil society. If every citizen contributed to the formation of *de facto* civil power in proportion to the quantity of his property, ownership would be assured. If an owner contributes less to the formation of *real* power in civil society than his property warrants, his possessions are in danger. I shall demonstrate this principle clearly; it explains the history of every revolution in human affairs. For the moment, however, I want to insist that church ownership has never possessed proper weight in the balance of political power, and consequently has never been solidly assured. This is truer now than ever [*App*., no. 4].

862. When necessary, therefore, the Church has the same sanction for its rights as all individuals and societies found in the natural state. This is an evident conclusion from the principles of rational Right, and altogether independent of ascertaining whether the Church wishes to use such a right, or thinks it in keeping with her spirit of generosity and meekness, or whether she judges its use prudent only at certain times and with certain qualifications, or has special instructions about the exercise of the right from her divine Founder — all this is completely outside the ambit of rational right and within the sole competence of divine, supernatural right.

863. According to natural right, therefore, the faithful under the leadership and direction of their pastors, and in addition to their status as citizens, have the right to unite and to deal peacefully with all matters pertaining to the jural defence of their rights and of the goods belonging to their society (the Church) in the same way as any other owner, just as universal-social right teaches.

864. The Church can also add spiritual penalties to support the defence of her own goods and rights, as she has always done. She defends herself in this way against those invested with civil

authority 'whatever their imperial or royal dignity', as the Council of Trent declares, if, under pretext of this power, 'however it may be exercised', they usurp these goods, or prevent their possession and use by those for whom they are destined, or change their purpose.[161] Such penalties are effective against Christians, but they cannot restrain avidity when faith is dead. They are non-violent sanctions, and hence cannot curtail the activity of violent people, but are most fitting for the Church, and the only penalties worthy of her.[162]

---

[161] Cf. sess. 22, *De Reform.*, c. 11.

[162] The following Councils protested and imposed penalties against usurpations at the time of the Merovingians: Clermont I, 535 AD, c. V; Orleans IV, 541 AD, c. 25; Orleans V, 549 AD, c. 14; Paris III, 557 AD, c. 2; Tours II, 567 AD, c. 24, 25. — After the 10th century, the following popes and councils protested and formulated laws against rulers disposing of the Church's temporalities: Council of Rheims, 1094 AD, c. 3, 4; Council of Rouen, 1050 AD, c. 10; Council of Tours, 1060 AD, c. 3; Council of Rome V, 1078 AD, c. I; Lateran Council I. 1123 AD, c. 14 (c. 14, c. 10, q. 1); Lateran Council II, 1139 AD, c. 10. — C. 3, c. 16, q. 2 (Nicol. II. 1059 AD); c. 1, c. 16, q. 7 (Gregor. VII, 1078 AD), c.3, *eod. Sive* c. 13, c. 1, q. 3 (*idem eod.*), Lateran Council II, 1139 AD, c. 19 — C. 17: 10, *De decim* (3, 30), c. 7: 10, *De praescript.* (2, 26), c. 9, 10. *De rer. permut.* (3, 19). — Lateran Council III, 1179 AD, c. 14. This decree is also found in c. 19: 10. *De decim.* (3, 30).

SECTION THREE

COMMUNAL RIGHT IN PERFECT THEOCRATIC SOCIETY

865. Certain matters connected with communal Right had to be dealt with in the preceding section on *governmental Right* in theocratic society. Similarly, the present section on *communal Right* will contain further points on governmental right that we have not yet been able to consider. These two aspects of right are strictly related, and cannot be worked out in isolation from one another. Many of their properties depend upon their mutual relationships.

866. *Communal Right* is the teaching about rights common to the faithful who make up the Church founded by Christ. This new society is open to all men and women without distinction precisely because it is the perfection and sublimation of human society. Those entering the Church are enriched with new rights of great nobility, and appear as new beings on earth clothed with an extraordinary dignity. Consciousness of this new dignity increases their intelligence and their natural aptitudes. It is not surprising therefore that baptised persons show a higher degree of *jural resentment* than usual. Feeling of this kind offers undoubted evidence of the existence and value of rights placed in being in the human person (cf. *RI*, 581–582), and indicates greater *foresight regarding the consequences of one's own actions*. In turn, such foresight expands the sphere of matters in which jural resentment manifests itself (cf. *RI*, 717–719). It is not to be wondered that Christians should have a unique appreciation of all their rights, including their temporal rights, which increases in value proportionately to the intelligence and interior dignity of the persons possessing them and injured by their violation. At the same time, Christians experience special repugnance at the moral deformity concomitant with the violation of rights, while appreciating the increased authority and rigour of the law upholding their worth. An *increase of jural*

resentment in the injured party, and of *remorse* in the offender, produces greater moral aversion to violation of the rights of others. In a word, all rights are observed more carefully and damaged more rarely. The society introduced into the world by JESUS Christ has thus changed mankind's jural state in two ways: 1. by conferring on human beings the new, supernatural rights and titles to rights proper to the new society; 2. by increasing the value and reinforcing the sanction of natural rights.

867. The increase in worth, and enhancement of the sanction of natural rights were the means by which Christ established more firmly the natural society of mankind, itself the initial sketch of the supernatural society he came to form. As we have said, the Church of JESUS Christ is only the perfect completion and sublimation of the human race considered as society.

If, in the course of this treatise on communal Right in perfect theocratic society, we were to explain all the changes in mankind's *jural state* when human beings enter the Church, the work would have to be divided into two parts. Part one would explain the rights proper to the faithful as such; part two would deal with the advantages and jural improvements of the rights common to mankind brought about by membership of the Church. The second part would open the way to a detailed description of the favourable influence of Christian religion on individuals, and on domestic and civil society. It would also show how the three species of uncertain, unprotected and forgotten rights proper to individuals, to domestic and to civil society, come to be ascertained, ensured and re-established by the foundation of Christ's theocratic society. Finally, it would indicate how the universal society of mankind, already lost in practical terms (cf. 638) because the human race had rejected common love of the supreme values (truth, virtue and virtuous happiness), was raised up and re-created in such a way that human beings were almost necessarily led to respect reciprocally the innate rights binding human society together.

All this, however, is excluded by the limited scope of this book. We have to be content with the few hints already expressed in our introduction where we showed that the appearance of Christianity on earth made human beings better suited as *subjects* of rights, and added new, effective value even to temporal rights (cf. 492–518). We simply add that the saving power of perfect theocratic society in relationship to the development and protection of the innate rights common to human beings (that is, the rights of initial theocratic society) is stronger than all human force and passion. Selfishness, material interests and great political power are all placed under duress and forced to serve mankind. World domination is permitted to grow and endure only on condition that it uses its power to protect the rights of universal society against injustices done by individuals and lesser societies.

868. As we said, *freedom* is one of the rights of the universal society of mankind (cf. *RI*, 65–66, 87–127), and the abolition of slavery, taking place under our eyes despite corrupt attempts to prevent it, is one of many clear examples of what we mean by saying that the rights of human society are safeguarded by theocratic society. Evidence for this is provided by the authoritative document of the commission on slavery set up by the King of France by decree of 20th May, 1840.[163] After considering the solid reasons for the abolition of slavery in the English colonies, the commission states that it can only be attributed to the action of the spirit of Christianity. This is all the more remarkable in so far as the irresistible influence of this spirit is active in nations separated from the body of the Church. We quote this extraordinary admission from persons who have studied all aspects of the question[164].

> It would be exaggerating or underestimating the role of the English government to assert that the abolition of the slave-trade and of slavery depended on its wisdom and foresight, or on its machiavellian policy. The English government neither took the initiative, nor directed events. It

[163] This commission was headed by the Duc de Broglie who, it seems, was responsible for the greater part of the report published by the Minister for the Marine and the Colonies (Paris, March 1843). The other members of the commission were: Count Saint-Criq, Marquis d'Audiffret, Rossi, peers of France; Count de Sade, Wustemberg, De Tracy, Ipp. Passy de Tocqueville, Bignon, Reinard, deputies; Baron de Mackau, Vice-Admiral, Count de Moges, Rear-Admiral, Filleau de Saint-Hilaire, Counsellor of State, Director of the Colonies; Jubellin, Commissary-General of the Navy; and Deputy Galos, Director of the Colonies.

[164] *Report* to Baron Roussin, Secretary of State for the Marine and the Colonies.

[868]

simply maintained the *status quo* until its hand was forced.
It systematically resisted the abolition of the slave-trade
for fifteen years,[165] and of slavery for another twenty-
five,[166] giving way only in the face of necessity.

It would also be exaggerating to say that philosophy and
philanthropy in England were mainly responsible for the
great undertaking. Philosophers and philanthropists certainly played their part in the battle, but the heat and
burden of the day was borne by the *religious spirit* that
provided the essential element for success. It was RELI-
GION which freed the blacks in the English colonies, by
raising up the likes of Clarkson, Wilberforce, Granville
Sharpe, and reinforcing their courage and unshakeable
perseverance. Religion gradually formed the great abolitionist party, first in the nation and then in Parliament. As
it grew and infiltrated all political parties, it obliged them
and, more importantly, the government to listen to it. For
forty years it forced its own point of view on all events and
circumstances, gradually winning the abolition of the
slave-trade in 1807.[167] Through its representatives it inspired the declarations of the Congresses of Vienna[168] and
Verona;[169] it drew up Buxton's motion in 1823, Canning's
resolution, Lord Bathurst's circular,[170] applied the Order in
Council of 2nd November to the colonies in 1831,[171] and
thus rendered inevitable the abolition of slavery in 1833;
and in 1838 the maintenance of the apprenticeship became
impossible.[172] The abolitionist party played a role in the fall
of the last Whig ministry in 1841, when it intervened to
prevent a reduction of the tax on sugar which might have
endangered the success of emancipation.

The abolitionist party has been as active in the colonies
as in metropolitan England: everywhere it has planted
churches, chapels, missions and congregations belonging

[165] 1792–1806.
[166] 1808–1833.
[167] *Acts*, 2nd May, 1807.
[168] *Declaration*, 8th February, 1815.
[169] *Declaration*, 28th November, 1822.
[170] *Circular*, 9th July, 1823.
[171] *Order in Council*, 2nd November (*Navy Publications*, p. 3–5, 1 vol. p. 151).
[172] *Parliamentary Debates*, 1841. Sittings of 7th, 10th, 11th, 12th, 13th, 14th, 17th, 18th May (*Navy Publications*, vol. 3, pp. 519–546).

to all the dissident sects of England[173] — It has worked to make emancipation necessary for London, and possible and easy in the Antilles,[174] by preparing the way, sowing the seed and overcoming all obstacles. Ministers of the established church, Methodists of all kinds, Presbyterians, Moravians, missionaries of the Society of London, Catholic priests and Baptist missionaries[175] have laboured consistently to penetrate workplaces and bring the light and consolation of the gospel to the Blacks. They have brought entire residential areas to their various communities, protecting slaves against their owners, and interceding with civil authority on behalf of oppressed classes. They have become beloved leaders, trusted arbiters and the true guardians of public order.

Sir Richard Hill, head of the Jamaican special magistrates,[176] says that despite the accusations against the missionaries emanating from high quarters during the Black rebellion of 1830, the colony owes more to their intervention than to that of the armed forces.

Events in the English colonies have something in common with the circumstances of the Roman empire as it moved towards decline. Beneath the surface of the old, narrow, oppressive society, established solely for the benefit of the ruling class, a Christian society began to grow, formed and protected by ministers of religion. Its components were the weak, the poor and the oppressed, but despite its initial ignorance it was progressive, ready to defend its position when the hour of freedom struck, and swift to recognise the voice of its leaders.[177]

The spirit of theocratic society is, therefore, capable of asserting and defending the natural rights of human society, and for this sublime purpose uses as its instruments, whether they like it or not, the ministers of communions separate from the Church, philosophers, philanthropists and the most powerful governments. All of them receive its light and are drawn to carry out its wishes, despite their initial reluctance.

---

[173] *Report on Jamaica*, Mr. Bernard (*Navy Publications*, vol. 3, p. 35).

[174] *Report on Antigua*, by the same author (*ibid*. p. 171).

[175] *Report on Jamaica*, Captain Layrle, 1840.

[176] Appendix to the *Report* of F. I. Lechevalier, 1st part, p. 97.

[177] Cf. *ibid*., pp. 118–119.

869. Despite their reluctance — but to everyone's advantage notwithstanding the 'violence' exercised over recalcitrant minds and hearts. One example will be sufficient to prove the point. Civil government resists the abolition of slavery for as long as possible, and only gives way to emancipation when forced to do so.[178] Nevertheless, it is the first to benefit in perfection, power and growth from the liberation of slaves who, because they are subject almost exclusively to domestic power, do not come under the influence of civil authority and remain extraneous to civil society. We shall show in our study of Right in civil society that an increase of power in domestic society entails a corresponding decline in the power of civil society because of a certain kind of disharmony between the two. How can civil society be perfectly vigorous when 'WE FIND EACH FAMILY A NATION', as Tacitus[179] *acutely observed about the conditions of his own time?*

870. The report previously cited continues:

> Everywhere the working class is in the majority, and subject to difficulties proportionate to its misery. Moreover, if enslaved, it does not depend directly upon public authority, but on the guardianship and control of its owners. Legally, slaves are things, not persons.[180] They are chattels in the city, and immobile possessions in the country. Public power does not normally interfere, except to moderate hardships caused by this legal fiction, and occasionally to restrict or protect seigniorial power.
>
> Deprived of civil rights and any share in social existence, slaves live on top of one another in all types of slum dwellings... each of which forms a society of its own, with its own way of life and its own development. These societies are subject to special rules, where justice is exercised, to a certain extent, according to particular forms. They become miniature States, with their own particular worship, prisons, kindergartens, hospitals and hospices for the old and infirm.
>
> Abolishing slavery means eliminating this multitude of

[178] This arises as in proportion to the influence that domestic society exercises over civil society.

[179] *Ann.*, 14, 44.

[180] To prove this, Articles 44, 45 of the edict of March, 1685, known as the *Black Code*, are cited here, but not Roman laws.

States within a State, and doing away with the fragmenta-
tion of sovereignty produced by competition between
public and domestic power. The abolition of slavery en-
sures the exercise of civil rights for the working class,
under the authority of common law and the immediate
protection of the judiciary. Social equality inevitably benefits
by such improvements.[181]

871. Civil society reaches perfection on condition that it is
open to as many as possible of the people coexisting within its
influence, whose share in the rights of the universal society of
mankind has to be freed from oppression and made effective.
This can only be brought about under the beneficent and unfailing influence of the perfect theocratic society founded by
Christ.

As it draws human beings to itself, theocratic society modifies
their temporal rights and ameliorates their jural state. This is its
first effect, about which we will speak later.

872. We have to say something about the *second effect*, that is,
the rights acquired by all on their entry into the Church. We
shall do this by adding what was omitted in the preceding
sections.

CHAPTER 1

The classification and the nature of the rights common to all the faithful

873. The rights proper to all the faithful composing the Church
can be divided into three classes:

1. those concerned with admission to the society;

2. those concerned with members already admitted amongst
the faithful;

3. accessory rights open to the faithful as members of the
human race, but occasioned by the Church to which they belong.

874. The nature of these rights can be sufficiently described in

---

[181] Cf. *Report*, pp. 72–73.

the following general terms. The right to belong to the Church, and the rights possessed by those already aggregated as members of the faithful, are individual, inalienable, and not subject to any kind of compromise. Discussion about them in society cannot be decided by majority vote, nor can they be diminished or dissolved by unanimous agreement.[182] Accessory rights can be changed, but only by the faithful possessing them, that is, the particular community or body holding them, in accord with the positive laws of the Church. They cannot be left to the discretion of a society having members not belonging to the Church (cf. *USR*, 266, 292), or not belonging to the body which holds the rights. This body, however, has to remain subordinate to legitimate superiors.

CHAPTER 2

Rights concerning admission to the Church

Article 1.
The right of admission relative to the person desiring admission, and to the Church bestowing admission

875. Granted the foundation of the Catholic Church by the Redeemer, every person deciding to believe what she proposes has the right, as we said, to be aggregated to the Church.

876. But has the Church any right relative to persons entering her society?

It is certain that all those coming to know the Church have the duty to join her as members. Although, in respect of God, this is a jural moral duty, it is only a moral duty relative to the faithful forming the Church militant on earth. A person not joining the body of the faithful does no injury to their rights. The Church, the community of the faithful (clergy and people), cannot demand entry on the part of non-members, although she has the right to use persuasion in calling all people to herself.

[182] Cf. *SP*, 219–220.

Article 2.
Can a member abandon church society?

877. A person who has freely entered the Church has no right to leave her.

878. This can be deduced in the first place from the perpetual nature of the society.

879. It can also be deduced from the nature of the aggregation which, while free (cf. 742) and presupposing free assent in human beings, renders obligatory the Right of seigniory and social Right, that is, governmental and communal right.

We have already seen that the Right of seigniory and Social right are fused in theocratic society (cf. 710–712). Entrance to such a society demands unending submission to divine dominion, and a consequent bond between self and God (cf. 742). Theocratic society also implies association between all those bonded in society with God (in Christ) (cf. 717–722). Admission of a believer to the body of the faithful under divine seigniory comes about through a contract in which the parties are the minister of the Church (who receives on behalf of the whole Church the request for entry), and the postulant. The Church's minister, as representative of the society, exercises an office belonging to governmental Right; the postulant brings communal Right into being through his promises.

The Right of seigniory comes into play as follows. In baptism, when admission to society takes place, God takes possession of the human being through an action exercised in his soul (cf. 738). The effect of this action is called by theologians the 'indelible character'. Through it, human beings are ordered to the worship of God. The basic stability of God's works prevents the dissolution of his domination within the human being, and of this intellectual encounter and effect impressed in the soul. The *bond of seigniory* put into effect once and for all on admission to the society cannot be dissolved. But is this true of the *social bond*?

880. The social bond can be dissolved *de facto*, but never *de iure* on the part of the member.

The social bond can be dissolved in fact whether the dissolution be viewed related to the bond a human being makes with God or with the Church. Neither God nor the Church wishes to retain in a society destined to benefit people those who of their own will renounce their place in that society. God wishes deiform society to be upheld through human freewill, because its only aim is voluntary honour of God on the part of human beings, the greatest good possible to a creature; for the same reason, the Church admits to communion in the good she possesses only those who wish freely and with true love to remain in her.

881. But if the matter is examined from the point of view of right, it is certain that no one entering theocratic society has the *right* to leave it. In virtue of the perpetual contract made on entry, members have promised to belong to it forever. This promise, an absolute condition of membership, has brought about the transfer to the Church of the members' *right* to remain perpetually united to her.

882. A person leaving the Church, therefore, harms the Church. Moreover, defection, far from diminishing the Church's rights over the member, increases them. As a result, those abandoning the Church are deprived of the good things inherent in her society, but they also remain subject to her authority. Her governmental Right is not lessened or weakened through the violation of that Right by her unfaithful members.

Article 3.
Can the Church separate members from the society?

883. When members fail to keep their promises and social agreements, a society can always deprive them of their share in the goods of the society (cf. *USR*, 458–466).

884. The Church does not take this step before using all the means in her power to bring back the faithful to the fulfilment of their obligations.

885. Depriving members of their share in the goods of a society is to exclude them from that society.

886. Nevertheless, the Church, while expelling those who obstinately refuse to carry out the obligations assumed in their social contract, never deprives them of hope of readmission. Indeed, she opens her doors to them whenever they ask, provided they repent of their unfaithfulness and are ready to give

her complete satisfaction — satisfaction which, we must remember, is wholly to their advantage.

887. Do persons expelled from the Church through their own fault regain by repentance a true right to be readmitted?

Yes, granted the superabundance of the charity of Christ who, in founding the Church, intended to found a society for people of good will, amongst whom are those who have returned to such a state by repenting of their faults.

888. The perpetual right of readmission to society after pacts with it have been broken is wholly characteristic of the Church of JESUS Christ, and is found in no other society.

CHAPTER 3

Rights proper to members of the faithful

889. We have distinguished three classes of Church rights: 1. her connatural rights relative to all human beings; 2. her connatural rights relative to her own members; 3. her acquired rights.

We could follow the same classification in dealing with the rights of individual members in the Church, but the Church's rights relative to mankind correspond with certain rights that all human beings have relative to the Church. These we have already examined (cf. 800–803). Although not proper to the faithful, they belong to them as members of the human race.

Consequently, we shall consider here only the *connatural* rights and *acquired* rights of the faithful.

Article 1.
The priesthood of the faithful, the source of their rights

890. Two things happen when an individual is aggregated to the Church (at baptism): 1. he is consecrated to divine worship and, through this consecration, sanctified, provided he places no obstacle to his sanctification; 2. a contract is established between God and the Church on one hand, and the individual who joins

the Church on the other (cf. 741–742). Consecration to divine worship is an interior operation wrought in the soul by God who invests the human being with a priestly character and dignity, later increased in confirmation and completed in holy orders.

891. The *priestly character* common to all the faithful[183] involves:

1. elevation of the human being to the supernatural order;

2. possession of the human being by the Lord, who destines the individual to his everlasting service in supernatural worship;

3. the faculty to carry out certain acts of supernatural worship, and to receive and exercise certain offices in the Church.

892. This faculty for carrying out acts of supernatural worship and exercising certain offices in the Church is the ESSENTIAL RIGHT of every member of the faithful. It is a CONNATURAL RIGHT (the FIRST RIGHT of its kind), given to the individual at the moment of his supernatural generation, that is, at baptism, and hence the source of every other right that a Christian possesses or can possess.

893. This *priestly character* has its source in God alone; it does not depend upon human will. The faculties that come with it cannot therefore be lost by the individual, although their exercise may be impeded.[184]

---

[183] 1 Pet 2: 9. The very early fathers of the Church speak of this first grade of priesthood common to all the faithful. St. Irenaeus (d. 201), *Contra Haereses, 4*, 20; Tertullian (d. 215), *De Orat., c.* 28; Origen (d. 234), *Hom. 9 in Levit.*, n. 9. The separated Greek Church has maintained the same teaching about the private priesthood shared by all the faithful, which it calls 'spiritual' or 'mystical' to distinguish it from the *sacramental priesthood* proper to priests alone; cf. *The Orthodox Confession*, Peter Mogilas, Bishop of Kiev (Ορθοδοξος ομολογια της κατολικης και αποστολικης εκκλησιας της ανατολικης, first published by Dragoman Panagiota, with a preface by the Patriarch Nectarius, and with a Latin translation, Amsterdam, 1662). This work, approved by four patriarchs and other bishops, states: 'The priesthood is of two kinds, one SPIRITUAL, the other SACRAMENTAL. All orthodox Christians enjoy the communion of the spiritual priesthood. — But the offerings are of the same kind as the priesthood, that is, prayers, thanksgiving, the rooting out of the evil desires and affections of the body; voluntary acceptance of martyrdom for the sake of Christ; and other things of this kind.' (p. 1, q. 708., Wratisl., 1751, in 8).

[184] Consequently, priests and prelates of the Church do not lose their

894. In virtue of this *character*, every member of the faithful shares in some way in each of the seven powers of the universal Church. He has (special) connatural rights relative to each of them, although he does not participate in them in the same way as those special persons invested with the *external priesthood* conferred in holy orders, when a more noble priestly character and dignity are bestowed. The external priesthood must never be confused with *interior*, first-level priesthood,[185] common to all the faithful, which could also be called *private, individual* priesthood to distinguish it from *public, social priesthood* conferred by the imposition of hands. The former indicates the individual's society with God; the latter the society between human beings associated with God.

895. The *acquired rights* of the faithful and their communities have ultimately the same source and principle. Let us see, therefore, how this individual, private priesthood gives the Christian a share in the seven priestly powers conferred by Christ on his Church, and how Christ has made the Christian capable of procuring other rights for himself.

authority, or the power of their ministry, by falling from the state of divine *grace*. The foundation of their *ecclesiastical power* is the *character* which they never lose. Bellarmine writes: 'I say, therefore, that an evil bishop or priest or teacher is a dead and not a true member of the Christ's body if we are speaking about the notion of a member as a living part of Christ's body', that is, in so far as he has broken the social contract, and lost social good; 'nevertheless he is a true member if we are speaking about the notion of instrument', that is, in so far as the operation by which God has united man to himself as his instrument — the source of the power of the character — never ceases. 'In other words, the pope and the bishops are true heads, and teachers are true eyes and true tongue of this body. This is the case because living members' — those sharing the life of Christ, which comprises the social good — 'are constituted through charity, which is lacking in the case of the impious who, however, are constituted as operative instruments through the POWER both of orders and jurisdiction' which finally is rooted in the order itself 'and which can exist without grace' (*De Ecclesia militante*, bk. 3, c. 9).

[185] The catechism of the Council of Trent speaking in the following terms calls these two kinds of priesthood 'interior' and 'exterior', p. 2, c. 7: 44–47. The heretics of the 16th century confused these two priesthoods, reducing them to a single thing. Cf. Council of Trent, sess. 23, c. 3.

Article 2.
How the simple faithful share in the seven powers left by
Christ to his Church

§1. *The faithful's share in the constitutive power*

896. People are enrolled in the Church when baptism is conferred according to the Church's intention. Properly speaking,
it is the bishop's right to confer baptism, but it may also be
administered validly by any person, whether belonging to the
Church or not.

If a member of the faithful baptises in case of necessity, he
exercises his *private priesthood*, and performs an act of greater
worship and dignity before God (although the effect on the
newly-baptised is the same) than that carried out by a person
not a member of the Church. Consequently, the well-disposed
Christian can gain special merit from his act.

§2. *The faithful's share in liturgical power*

897. With regard to liturgical power, the faithful as such do not
possess the faculty of *immolating* the victim of the New Testa-
ment through the consecration of bread and wine, but they have
the *faculty of offering that victim* to the eternal Father.

898. In addition, they have the faculty of *immolating* themselves by their union in spirit with the victim of propitiation for
the world's salvation. The Christian's self-immolation comes
about through his sacrificial love, which keeps him constantly
prepared to undergo actual death for the sake of witness to
Christ, for justice and the increase of God's kingdom.

899. In the same way all the prayers and actions offered to
God by the faithful acquire special efficacy and value through
the priestly character with which the faithful are invested by
God himself.[186]

---

[186] The *Catechism of the Council of Trent* speaks in the following terms of
the functions proper to the interior, private priesthood, possessed by all the

900. The *power of consecration*, which constitutes external, public, ministerial priesthood, includes the power to *bless* and consecrate all things. In virtue of this power everything is directed in an ordered way to human salvation through divine action. The *character* impressed on all the baptised does not give them the power to bless, properly speaking, but to receive the effects of the Church's blessings, and to benefit by the use of blessed objects, or sacramentals.

§3. *The faithful's share in eucharistic power*

901. In virtue of their baptism, the faithful acquire the right to receive the other sacraments.

Above all, they share in eucharistic power because the priestly character enables them to receive the holy Eucharist and the graces flowing from this sacrament, if they place no obstacle to them.

902. In case of necessity, they can also administer this sacrament to themselves and to other baptised persons.

---

faithful: 'As far as the interior priesthood is concerned, all the faithful are priests after they have been washed in the saving water. This is particularly the case with the just who have the spirit of God and have been made true members of JESUS Christ by the gift of divine grace. These immolate spiritual sacrifices to God on the altar of their heart through faith inflamed by charity. Such offerings are in general all good and decent actions which are done with reference to the glory of God. Hence we read in the book of the Apocalypse: "Christ has freed us from our sins by his blood, and made us a kingdom, priests to his God and Father" (Apoc. 1: 5–6). In the same way, the prince of Apostles has said: "Like living stones be yourselves built into a spiritual house, to be a holy priesthood, to offer spiritual sacrifices acceptable to God through JESUS Christ" (1 Pet 2: 5). The Apostle also exhorts us to present our bodies as a living sacrifice, holy and acceptable to God, which is our spiritual worship (cf. Rom 12: 1). Long before, David had said: "The sacrifice acceptable to God is a broken spirit; a broken and contrite heart, O God, you will not despise" (Ps 51: 17). All these things are easily understood as applicable to the interior priesthood' (*Catechism of the Council of Trent*, p. 2, *De ordinis sacramento*, n. 23).

§4. *The faithful's share in the power to bind and loose,*
and in the healing power

903. In virtue of the *character*, the faithful can receive the sacrament of penance and be absolved from their sins.

904. For the same reason, the Church can exercise her power to bind the faithful, by retaining their sins without absolution, or by holding them under her censures.

905. The faithful can also receive the healing sacrament of extreme unction, which confers grace when no obstacle is placed in its path. This sacrament, too, operates in virtue of the priestly character impressed on souls as a fruitful seed of grace.

§5. *The faithful's share in the hierogenetic power*

906. Where a matrimonial contract exists between Christians according to the conditions required by the Church,[187] the baptismal *character* enables this covenant to represent the union between Christ and his Church and to bestow grace corresponding to such a union. In a word, the Christian marriage-contract is also a sacrament.

907. Consequently, their priestly character makes Christians *ministers* of this sacrament (this is the more usual opinion amongst theologians, and one I hold as certain). Although the character bestows on the faithful only a passive faculty to receive other sacraments, it gives them an active faculty to administer and effect that of marriage [*App.*, no. 5].

---

[187] When the Church establishes certain formalities, such as the presence of the parish priest and two witnesses, for the validity of the sacrament of matrimony, she decides and determines only the *matter* of the sacrament. The matter of the other sacraments has been precisely determined by their divine Founder, but in marriage JESUS Christ has indicated it only in part by deciding that it must be a *monogamous* contract between baptised persons. He has allowed the Church to regulate the formalities which at various times render marriage a legitimate contract worthy to represent the union of Christ and his Church. These formalities thus become matter worthy of such a sacrament.

[903–907]

§6. The faithful's share in the teaching power

908. Although preaching the gospel is a responsibility proper to bishops, and priests missioned by bishops, the ordinary members of the faithful are also called in part to the ministry of the word because:

1. They are obliged to confess JESUS Christ before others when the Saviour's glory requires this.[188]

909. 2. They can enunciate teaching received from the pastors of the Church, and under their direction communicate it to others by word or in writing (the office of teacher or writer).

910. 3. They sometimes find themselves in circumstances obliging them to hand on their faith. Parents, for example, have a duty to instruct their children in sound doctrine not only through others, but often as part of their own everyday life.

911. 4. The faithful also have the right to compare the teaching of an individual pastor with that of other pastors in the universal Church, and to reject the former if it is contrary to the decisions expressed by the universal Church, or to choose the most common, authoritative opinion in the case of doubtful matters.[189]

912. This last right, common to all the faithful, is also the source of rights in civil authority, or rather in persons invested with such authority. As members of the faithful wishing to direct themselves rightly in their private and public lives, they can investigate the doctrine of the universal Church by comparing the teaching of individual pastors with decisions of ecumenical councils and the global consent of tradition.

913. It is clear, therefore, that certain abstract rights claimed for civil authority by modern publicists are erroneous and without foundation. An example is the *jus reformandi* which, according to some modern authors, consists in the faculty of deciding whether the Church is to be admitted into a State, and under what conditions. This 'right', however, is a consequence of the misuse of the word 'Church' by Protestants. If the

---

[188] The *character* impressed on the faithful by the sacrament of confirmation forms and disposes them in a special way to profess their faith courageously before the whole world.

[189] Cf. *SP*, 476–486.

Church is one, as it is defined in the apostolic creed and recognised by Catholics, non-Catholic bodies cannot truly call themselves 'churches' without abusing the word. It is absurd to maintain that civil authority has the responsibility of deciding to permit the true Church into a State. Those exercising this authority, together with all citizens making up civil society, have a manifest *duty* to admit the true Church, and hence have no *right* to refuse it entrance.[190]

914. Relative to the true Church and her teachings, civil authority has no other rights than those of the faithful. That is: the right to verify the existence of the true Church in order not to confuse her with misleading, false churches; the right to know the dogmatic decisions of the true Church; the right to compare the teaching of individual pastors and masters with dogmatic decisions of the Church; the right to acknowledge legitimate pastors and distinguish them from intruders. The rights of civil authority go no further than this; and at this point its duties begin.[191]

[190] Restoring the *correct use* of language is one of the means of helping towards mutual understanding in many difficult matters. The introduction of defective language has certainly been instrumental in leading the world to falsify many ideas. The word 'religion', for example, has been applied to all 'superstitious beliefs', and the word 'Church' to indicate communions separate from the Church. Using these two words to indicate the opposite of what they mean has produced all kinds of fallacious reasoning. Theodosius spoke out on behalf of accurate logic as well as justice when he decreed that only those should be called 'Catholics' who held the teachings of Pope Damasus and of Peter, Bishop of Alexandria. Others were to be called 'heretics', and their assemblies were forbidden to name themselves 'Churches' (bk. 2, *Cod. Theod., De Fide Catholica*, 28th February, 380). For a description of the sophisms arising from the application of the word 'religion' to all superstitious beliefs, cf. my *Frammenti d'una storia dell'impietà* (*Apologetica*, p. 326 ss.).

[191] For example, in times of schism. J. Schell writes: 'Before the schism under Urban VI (1378–1389) there were scarcely any signs of such [royal] *placets*. And even in unhappy times, for the sake of caution, we see this right exercised so that the bulls of the true pope might be distinguished from those of the anti-popes. Consequently, when the cause ceased, the exercise of the royal *placet* also ceased' (In his additions to the *Institutiones Juris Ecclesiastici P. Mauri Schenkl* (§364, B). — J. Jung, (*Orig. hist. iuris sacro. commentar.*) showed that there is no example of the modern *placet regio* prior to the 16th century. Its origin is to be found in the Protestant *territorial system* which

[914]

915. It may indeed be the case that civil authority has a *jus reformandi* relative to communions outside the Church, but such a right must be exercised non-violently. Violence is to be reserved for the repression of crime or wrong doing against ownership, or attempted violations of ownership. Some communions separated from the Church, have, however, surrendered themselves totally to the exercise of civil power, which thus acquires special rights over them.[192]

916. Because of their priestly character, Christians have a special aptitude or right to exercise these actions, relative or analogous to teaching power in the Church, and can obtain corresponding merit through the grace accompanying them.

§7. The faithful's share in the ordinative power

917. Certain matters in the Church and its government have already been determined by her Founder and are therefore unchangeable.

Others remain to be determined by the wisdom of the teaching Church, assisted by the Holy Spirit, according to the needs of the times. A general name for such directives is 'church discipline', the sphere within which ordinative power evolves.

918. Power over church discipline has been entrusted in its fullness to the head of the Church. It is held in a subordinate manner by the bishops, who exercise it in part through their priests. Finally, the ordinary faithful have some share in it, and this we must now describe.

subjects the Church to the government of a territorial lord.

[192] The following is the sense in which *jus reformandi* was introduced in the treaty of Osnabrück (art. 5, §30): 'The sovereign is granted the faculty of examining his subjects' profession of faith in order to acknowledge and accept it when it accords with the true Catholic faith. If it does not so accord, he can amend it according to justice and prudence.' In this sense, there is no absurdity in such a right. The civil authority, however, cannot lay claim even to *jus cavendi* related to *essential matters of religion* such as dogma, dogmatic formulae, and morality. There is no danger to the public good from such things. Cf. *Institutiones juris ecclesiastici Mauri de Schenkl*, §361, Landishut, 1830.

919. The faithful have a right to influence, and to a certain extent do influence, the government of the Church in determined ways recognised and accepted by the pastors of the Church. Their influence extends to the choice of *persons* for the government of the Church, to disciplinary *laws*, and to church *temporalities*.

These are the three objects to which are referred the influence that all the faithful can exercise in the ordinative power of the Church.

A.
The influence of the faithful in the choice of persons
for office in the Church

920. Although the people have no right to choose and appoint their own pastors — this is proper to the clergy — they have a right to be given acceptable pastors enjoying their esteem and trust.

921. From very early days in the Church's history, the local bishops and clergy would assemble with the people of the diocese to choose a new bishop for the vacant see. The people's presence on such an occasion helped to indicate the person enjoying their esteem and trust. Generally speaking, the bishops' chief responsibility was to judge doctrinal soundness in the candidate; the local clergy bore witness to the candidate's holiness and prudence; and the people showed their esteem and trust in the person proposed as their pastor and father. The qualities required in a good pastor capable of ruling the people are in fact: *sound doctrine, holiness, prudence, and the weight of public opinion.*[193]

922. The Christian people's right to pastors they trust is inalienable. Sovereigns holding nomination to vacant sees are obliged to respect it.[194]

[193] Cf. Thomassin, p. 2, bk. 2, c. l; De Marca, bk. 8, c. 2, ss. Van Epsen, p. 1, tit. 13, c. l; and the important work of the brothers Lamennais on the appointment of bishops.

[194] St. Alphonsus de' Liguori shows that popes and kings SIN MORTALLY when they appoint worthy, but not THE MOST WORTHY, candidates to the episcopate. He says the same about benefices with cure of souls. 'We have to

923. The *choice* of a pastor in the Church is accompanied by a *test* destined to show that he is not unworthy of the office to which he is called. This process is the responsibility of the bishops of the province and the pope, but all the faithful can act as witnesses.[195]

924. The people are also invited to reveal matters indicating unworthiness in a candidate suggested for promotion to sacred orders. This is the reason for announcing the names of ordinands from the pulpit.[196]

925. If a pastor is unfortunately guilty of serious misdemeanours through neglect of his sacred obligations, the faithful can appeal to superior hierarchic power in the Church for a remedy to this deplorable state of affairs.[197]

---

distinguish between benefices with cure of souls and simple benefices. If we are dealing with the former, it is certain that patrons of episcopates, such as rulers, are held to this.' Again: 'There is no doubt whatsoever... that in cases of benefices with cure of souls, the patron, even if a lay person, is gravely bound to present the most worthy candidate' (*Th. M.* bk. 4, 91–111).

[195] C. 8, d. 64 (Council of Nicea, 325 AD). — C. 3, d. 65 (Council of Antioch, 332 AD). — C. 6, d. 61 (Council of Laodicea, 372 AD). — C. 5, d. 65 (Council of Carthage II, 390 AD). — C. 2, §3, d. 23 (*Statuta eccles. antiq.*). — Innocent. I, *epist.* 24, *ad Alexandr. episc. Antioch.* 451 AD, c. 1 (Schaenemann, *Epist. Rom. Pontif.* t. 1, p. 603). — Council of Chalcedon, 431 AD, c. 28. — Damas. *epist.* 8, *ad Achol.* 380 AD, c. 1, 3; *epist.* 9, *ad eund.*, c. 2 (Schaenemann, p. 366–69). — Council of Constantinople, *epist.* 13, *ad Damas.* 382 AD, c. 5, 6 (Schaenemann, p. 396). — Boniface, *epist.* 15 *ad episc. Maced.* 422 AD, c. 6 (Schaenemann, p. 746). — Leo the Great, *epist.* 69, 70, 104, 122, 129, 130, ed. Baller.

[196] Church law on this matter is found in the Roman Pontifical: 'Those who are to be raised to major orders will go to the bishop a month before ordination. He will order the parish priest, or anyone else whom he may see fit, to make careful enquiries from people worthy of faith about the place and date of birth of the ordinands, their morals and their life, after their names and desire to be ordained have been publicly displayed in the church. The person nominated by the bishop will send testimonial letters containing the result of the enquiries as soon as possible' (*De ordinibus conferendis*).

[197] 'The pope (Alexander II) sent legates to Milan in order to eradicate the disturbances (1067 AD) once and for all. The legates promulgated constitutional rules and saw that they were observed. At the same time, enlightened persons took a stand against the objections arising from ignorance, or rather from licence and obstinacy. Such an objection, lying at the root of great abuses, was the claim of some bishops that their subjects had no power to accuse them. Truly learned men took exactly the opposite point of view and

926. Through their generosity and pious endowments, the faithful acquire certain other rights regarding choice of persons for church office. However, this is not the place for a study of rights connected with *patronage* in so far as they are already determined by positive laws, although we must at least indicate some that follow from rational Right.

927. Church ministries can be divided into those involving the care of souls, and those not involving it.

928. If a member of the faithful founds and endows out of his own pocket an ecclesiastical office unconnected with the cure of souls, equity requires that the choice of persons in charge of the work should be left to the founder, if he so wishes, provided that the bishops in charge of local churches recognise the candidate as not unworthy, and suitable for the work.

929. The case is different where there is question of the cure of souls or a public office.[198] Divine as well as rational Right

maintained that in the case of suspicion it was completely reasonable to require bishops and lower churchmen to show their innocence or humbly to confess their guilt. St. Peter was reproved by St. Paul, his inferior. If prelates could not be judged, no one would willingly submit to canon law. If children of the Church could not say a word against their pastor (there would scarcely be witnesses to his behaviour outside the parish), the way would be open to all kinds of unreproved licence and to the destruction of discipline (P. Dam., bk. 2, ep. 12). Henrion, *Storia universale della Chiesa*, bk. 32.

[198] The spirit of the Church requiring freedom for bishops in their appointment of priests to the cure of souls, and the way in which such freedom was filched from the Church, can be seen by examining the origin of lay nomination to benefices with cure of souls. One of the origins of this patronal right was the existence of private oratories required by the great landowners for themselves and their serfs. Private oratories naturally provided a kind of private service, and it was fitting that the choice of priest should be left to the owner who maintained the chapel. The Church simply reserved the right to see that unworthy priests were excluded. The gentry's right relative to their *private worship* passed over to *public worship*, however, when population-increase changed these private chapels into parish churches. The proprietor's successors maintained their right of nomination to the parish although they sometimes no longer possessed the territory comprising it. Decr. p. 2, caus. 16, q. 7, c. 35 (*Capit. Ludov. P.* 829 AD, c. 2); c. 36 (Council of Trier, 895 AD); q. 1, c. 59 (*Capit. 1, Car. Magni.* 803 AD, c. 1); *ibid. Corr. Rom.* The word 'owners' is relative to 'tenants'. Ecclesiastics appointed to chapels established on estates by landowners were compared to 'tenants'. Cf. c. un. C. Th., *ne colon. inscio domino* (5, 11); c. un. C. Th. *de colon. Thrac.* (2, 51).

requires the best and *most suitable* person available for the work. The faithful are not competent to judge which of the candidates is the *most suited*; this falls under the responsibility of the churches' rulers. Again, long experience shows that members of the faithful are subject to human passion, to partiality and to opinions that do not give sufficient guarantee for presuming that their nominations will take account of the *most worthy* and *suitable* subjects for office. Moreover, if a benefice is at stake, there is greater danger of violating the divine Right requiring the best candidate. Benefactors will perhaps prefer priests of their own families to enjoy the material advantages of the foundation, with grave, consequent danger of children without a call being forced by ignorant parents into the ecclesiastical state.

930. It would seem that the right to nominate to such offices could be entrusted to faithful of great virtue and wisdom only in exceptional cases. The right would have to be strictly personal, as required by reason and the spirit of the Church, and non-transferable. Descendants of a person holding such a right offer diminishing guarantees to the Church in so far as their suitability is unknown.[199]

931. Nevertheless, there could be such a scarcity of churches and priests that the public good might seem to demand the foundation of churches and pastoral offices with right of nomination in the benefactors, if there were no other way of satisfying requirements. If this were the only way of providing for the Christian people, it would certainly be a lesser evil to have suitable rather than the most suitable persons in the care of

---

[199] The right to nominate ecclesiastics to churches does not appear in the Church until the 5th century when bishops in Gaul who founded churches in other dioceses were granted the faculty of choosing priests for this work (c. 10, Council of Orange, 441 AD; Council of Arles. 452 AD, c. 39). This raised no difficulty; the right invested in the bishop was simply personal. Until the 5th century, lay founders were not given the enjoyment of this right, which they obtained in the 6th century, but even then it was granted only on personal grounds, without their being able to transmit it to their successors (cf. *Nov. Just.*, c. 2, nov. 123, c. 18. — *Decreti*, p. 2, c. 16, q. 1, c. 31 (Pelagius I, c. 557 AD); — *idem cod.*, c. 18, q. 2, c. 4, 30; — Council of Toledo IX, 655 AD, c. 16, q. 7, q. 92).

souls. Such circumstances explain in part the present growth of church discipline.

However, although the Church's favourable consideration of such a case appears justified in the circumstances outlined, as far as she is concerned, there is on the other hand no justification for the patron to demand such an unreasonable right as a condition of his generosity, provided he is instructed about the right and its underlying principle which requires the most worthy and suitable priests for the care of souls. Such a principle can best be put into practice only when the clergy themselves make the choice [*App.*, no. 6].

B.
The faithful's influence over disciplinary legislation
in the Church

932. Although the pastors of the Church have exclusive power, not shared with the faithful, to make obligatory laws, and to impose morally obliging commands, the faithful subject to this legislation rightly influence these disciplinary requirements, with the consent of the pastors themselves. The reason for this indirect influence, and the limits of its extension, are clarified in the following propositions.

933. *1st proposition.* All the faithful are obliged to desire the greater good of the Church, even at the cost of some material damage to themselves.

This is evident, just as it is evident that the greater good is to be preferred to the lesser good, public good to private good, and moral good to every other good.

934. On the other hand, it is certain that moral good can sometimes be in collision with material good. This, however, is only accidental, in the sense that the complex of effects obtained in seeking the greater good will also bring about indirectly, and perhaps unexpectedly, greater temporal good.

935. *2nd proposition.* The Church's government alone is responsible for deciding which laws and directives are for the

greater good of the Church. The faithful are obliged to obey these commands.[200]

Two reasons will suffice to prove the point. First, governments are always the competent judge of what serves the society they administer.[201]

936. Second, the faithful must believe that church government is divinely assisted, and therefore worthy of their confidence.

937. *3rd proposition.* The faithful have the right and duty to know church laws and directives, and to distinguish them from those which pass as such. Similarly, they have to compare them in cases of collision, and follow those emanating from higher authority. In a word, they have the right to know the true, obligatory will of the Church in order to fulfil it.

There is no need here to demonstrate this. The faithful's duty of obedience is sufficient to bestow these rights upon them.

938. *4th proposition.* If churchmen abuse their power by employing it in their own interest, each member of the faithful and each society has the right to self-protection against material damage. No one, however, has the right to judge rashly, or to regulate his conduct according to harmful suspicion, or to fail in obedience towards authentic church laws and precepts, or to demand safeguards which exceed the right to protection (cf. *RI*, 1820–1900).

939. *5th proposition.* Although the government of the Church is the sole competent judge of the greater good accruing to the Church from ecclesiastical laws and directives, and hence solely responsible for such dispositions, the Church sincerely desires such good to be obtained without prejudice to the temporal welfare of the faithful, or at least with as little prejudice as possible. But the competent judges of the possible damage are, in this case, the faithful themselves, or the civil government

---

[200] Civil authority is simply the authority of lay people regulated by an administration. Lay faithful invested with civil government can, of course, regulate the rights of individuals subject to them, but not increase the sum of these rights. Hence the truth of the proposition is affirmed by sound canonists: 'The civil power has no deliberative right over essential or accidental religious headings in matters proximately relating to the salvation of souls' (Maurus von Schenkl, *Institutiones Juris ecclesiastici*, §360).

[201] On the duty members have to depend in these matters upon the judgment of government in their society, cf. *SP*, 122.

acting for them (cf. *RI*, 610). The faithful, and the civil government representing them, act according to their right and in conformity with the intention of the Church herself when protesting to the Church about temporal harm resulting from church directives. Similarly they may, together with the Church, add conditions which avoid temporal harm without loss to spiritual good.

940. This proposition shows:

1. The error of politicians and publicists who maintain that the Church's rights have been satisfied when she has been granted the faculty of making arrangements in essential matters of religion, that is, in those matters without which she could not even continue to exist. The Church's right is not restricted to satisfying the *necessities* of the faithful; it extends to what *helps* them reach the sanctity and perfection of their Gospel call, which must be given preference to temporal matters.

941. 2. That the faithful, and civil governments acting on their behalf, can hold discussions with ecclesiastical government for the purpose of qualifying and re-arranging disciplinary dispositions that could harm temporal welfare. They must do this in good faith, however, not for the sake of disputing with the Church or harming her. And they must suffer in peace.

942. 3. That although the faithful have no right to know and examine church dispositions before they are published (this could harm the greater good of the Church by causing delay and other difficulties in the presentation of ecclesiastical directives), church authorities are obliged to consult the faithful if disciplinary dispositions seem harmful to their temporal welfare. The faithful are competent in their own temporal affairs, and their advice and judgment should be considered. Similarly, authority should take in good part the complaints of the faithful, and evaluate them carefully in all good faith. If the desired modifications are compatible with the greater good of the Church, they should be accepted.

C.
The faithful's influence on church temporalities

943. We have already seen that relative to temporalities, the clergy have two principal rights:

    1. to be maintained by the faithful;

    2. to acquire temporalities in the name of the Church, and of the faithful in need, under just titles which allow all individuals and societies to exercise ownership, according to the conditions agreed between Church and State.

The first right rests upon a title proper to the clergy; the second depends upon titles common to all citizens.

944. Relative to the first title, the faithful, the community of the faithful, have the right not to give more than is sufficient for the maintenance of the clergy.

945. Relative to common titles, the faithful community must allow them to subsist. It cannot extinguish them without harm to the clergy and to church society.

946. Granted the existence of church temporalities acquired under just titles, according to rational Right, the faithful have or can acquire two rights in their regard:

    1. the right of administration;

    2. the right of calling in aid.

a)
The right of administration

947. The right of administration can be held or acquired by the faithful within the limits or titles outlined in the following norms:

    1st norm. Temporalities destined for the maintenance of the clergy and of worship must of their nature be administered by the clergy themselves, unless testators or donors have indicated otherwise.

948. *2nd norm.* Temporalities destined for works of charity must be administered by the corporations formed of persons benefiting by the works, or by those lawfully acting on their

behalf. These representatives have almost always been the pastors of the Church,[202] unless testators or donors have indicated otherwise.

949. *3rd norm.* The clergy, that is, those holding authority in church government, always have the duty and the right to see that these temporalities are used for the purpose intended, and to demand an account of stewardship from administrators,[203] unless the testators and donors have indicated otherwise.[204]

950. *4th norm.* Because the will of a donor is an obligatory law, the faithful appointed by the donor have the right to administer goods destined for pious works.

951. *5th norm.* If a pious legacy cannot be executed in the present or future, it seems that rational Right would indicate its passing to the designated heir, or the necessary heir. If there is

[202] At first, the Apostles themselves administered the offerings of the faithful; later, they did this through deacons (cf. Acts 6[: 1–6]); later still bishops were administrators, according to the prescriptions of the canons (*Can. Apostol.* 40: 1, *Praecipimus*, etc. c. 7 and 8. — Council of Grangra, 333 AD, c. 24 and 25. — Council of Antioch, 345 AD, c. 22. — Council of Agde, c. 25, — Council of Orleans I, *relat.* c. 32, *causs.* 12, *q.* 2, etc., *7 causs.* 10. *q.* 1, etc. etc.). Sometimes, however, they allowed the beneficiaries to administer the offerings for themselves (cf. Thomassin, pt. 3, bk. 2, c. 1–12; and bk. 3, c. 1).

[203] Cf. Council of Trent, sess. 22, *De Reformat.*, c. 8. Supreme supervision over such goods belongs of its nature to the head of the Church; the popes have always legislated in cases of pious benefices and their administration. Pope Simplicius (457 AD) decided the equitable division of church temporalities, or perhaps renewed it (*Epis. 3, ad episcopos Florentium, Equitium et Severum*). Pope Gelasius did the same a short time later (*Ep. 9 ad episcopos Lucaniae*; cf. Rupprecht, *Not. 1 in ius can.* bk. 3, tit. 5, n. 8). Other examples of similar arrangements can be found in Gufi (*Vindic. Iurium Stat. Eccl.*, pt. 1, n. 133 ss.), in the *Decretals* under the title *De Rebus Ecclesiae alienandis vel non*, and in the extraordinary constitution *Ambitiose*. Protestants themselves have acknowledged the usefulness of this papal right, and affirm that the popes have often been responsible for preventing the alienation of church temporalities (cf. Plank, *Geschichte der Christlich-Kirchl. Verfassung*; cf. bk. 2, *Abth.* 2, *Abschn.* 3, 386). This right was also solemnly acknowledged by the Apostolic See, and by recent concordats (French concordat, 1801, art. 13; Bavarian concordat, art. 8).

[204] The Church's respect for the desires of testators is such that she renounces the right of inspecting the administrative accounts of pious bequests when founders or donators require this. Cf. Council of Trent sess. 22, *De Reformat.*, c. 9.

no heir, or the work cannot be continued after the death of the heir, it would seem right and wholly in keeping with equity and piety that the Church, in her own name and that of the community of the faithful, assign the temporalities to some other good work in accordance with the presumed intention of the benefactor. In such a case, when temporalities are without an owner, it can certainly be presumed that a Christian wishing to act charitably would leave the decision in these circumstances to the pastors of the Church.

b)
The right to call in aid

952. The right to defend the Church and her temporalities is proper not only to the faithful but to all human beings (cf. *RI*, 267). Such a right is a beneficence, and every individual has the right to benefit others (cf. 802).

953. This right is limited and conditioned, however, by the will of the Church. Individuals and societies have no right to protect and defend the Church and her temporalities in cases where the Church *does not want them to do so.* Moreover, where the Church wishes to be defended, *the way in which she wishes to be defended* must be respected. The Church is the sole judge competent to decide when and how protection, defence and calling in aid, together with acts dependent upon such titles, assist or harm her.

954. The greatest injustices have always been committed in the name of right. The imperfect description of rights provided by publicists leaves a gaping hole, not a tiny crack, open to human ill-will. A vague, abstract right, isolated from its limits and conditions, is not a right. Or, if it is a right, it is also a very satisfactory vehicle for human injustice carried out by people believing (or pretending to believe) they have no obligations to keep to the limits and conditions of the right simply because they proclaim it without limits or conditions. This explains the Church's miserable enslavement to persons who, while boasting

of their right to protect[205] her under the pretext of their right to
be called in as aid, oppress her in so many ways and expropriate
her temporalities. There is no unlimited, unconditional right to
protect and defend the Church; the only existing right depends
upon the Church's willingness regarding the occasions and
means of exercising it.

955. This vile abuse of the sacred right to protection and
calling in aid was strengthened as it became a positive, permanent[206] office attached to dignities or families. In such cases, the
quality of the person holding the office was always in doubt: he
might be good or bad, just or unjust, prudent or imprudent. In
addition, when such offices became permanent in families, or
connected with dignities, the abuses became customs which
then displaced laws and right. Yet there were times when lack of

---

[205] Cf. *Esposizione dei sentimenti di Sua Santità (Pius VII) alla dichia-
razione dei principi e Stati protestanti riuniti dalla confederazione germanica.*
'His Holiness is aware of the extent to which German publicists push the
supreme rights of protection over the Church (we need not mention other
reasons). He knows that this protection has been a pretext for attributing
unlimited powers *circa sacra* to rulers, power unknown to our forebears and
opposed to the divine prerogatives of the hierarchy.'

[206] 'Calling in aid' had two purposes, one *peaceful*, the other *warlike*. The
former was intended to assist the Church before the *civil courts*, to exercise
civil jurisdiction in the name of the Church, or to help churches with *economy*
and financial administration; the second undertook to defend church rights
against violence and obtrusion. We must therefore distinguish 'robed calling
in aid' and 'armed calling in aid.'

'Robed calling in aid' was 1. *forensic*, and as such divided into assistance
given in civil disputes, and assistance in jurisdiction, rendered by exercising
on behalf of churches the jurisdiction they possess; 2. *economic*; 3. *total* or
partial; 4. *basic*, or *delegated*; 5. *unshared*, in so far as the founders reserved
it for themselves, or *chosen* and *planned*, in so far as churches asked for it
under the form of pact, or *granted*, in so far as the ruler exercised it for
churches without being asked; 6th *hereditary*.

'Armed calling in aid' was 1. *universal*, and as such exercised by emperors
from Charlemagne onwards in defence of the Apostolic See and the Catholic
Church; 2. *governmental*, that is, part of Catholic civil government. The
second kind of 'armed calling in aid' is either *general* or *special*, that is, either
the natural duty of protecting the Church incumbent upon government by
Catholics, or the duty arising from obligations incurred by rulers or others
as a result of treaties, oaths, etc. 3. The final division of 'armed calling in aid'
is that of *simple protection*. Cf. *Institutiones Juris Ecclesiastici*, Fr. Maurus von
Schenkl, Landishut, 1830, §386.

[955]

organisation in civil society, or bad organisation, made defence and protection of the weak an urgent necessity. In periods like this it seemed imperative to depend for security on extraordinary, exceptional and extra-social protection; privileges seemed to afford greater safeguards than imperfect, inefficacious common laws.

956. So it came about that

> organised aid, once necessary for the well-being and benefit of the Church, often resulted in almost fatal harm to her. Those called in aid abandoned their offices as protectors to become masters, whose rights they exercised by tyrannising churchmen and usurping temporalities under cover of lawful salaries[207]… they impoverished churches with their banqueting and their extortionate demands, corrupted the morals of the people, arbitrarily delegated their own duties to others, mortgaged, enfeoffed and sold their offices, and so on. Church authorities did all they could to free their churches from such assistance. Such freedom was considered a great benefaction, and begged as a favour from emperors and princes.[208] In particular, church authorities found assistance at lower levels particularly harmful, especially in the 11th century. It was eventually abolished by Frederick II and Hadrian III.[209]

CHAPTER 4

Accessory and occasional rights in Church society — Christianity

957. The Church militant is one because she has one invisible head, one visible head, one faith, one baptism, and one Spirit animating and uniting her through charity in a single family with God, her sole Father. Her obligations are identical; her internal means of action (grace) is the same for all, her hope and

[207] Such salaries were called *advocaticum, advocatia, advocatio, advocatiae justitiae*. Cf. Du Fresne, *Glossarium*, under 'advocatia'.

[208] Cf. Gallade, *Diss. de Advocatis Eccl.*, c. 6, §12; Van Espen., *I. E. univ.*, pt. 2, tit. 25, c. 1, n. 26 ss.

[209] Fr. Maurus von Schenkl, *Institutiones Juris Ecclesiastici*, §386.

her end the same. But she is an organic body, made up of different members and organs, each of which is composed of several individual persons. Consequently, there are many subjects of right in the Catholic Church. They can be enumerated as follows:

1. The universal Church in its totality, with the pope as its head, is a subject of right.

2. The clergy (the teaching Church) in its totality, with the pope at its head, is a subject of rights.

3. All the faithful (including churchmen in their role as members of the faithful) are a subject of rights.

4. The clergy are divided into various bodies such as dioceses, parishes, special ecclesiastical and religious societies. All these bodies are particular subjects of rights.

5. Every clerical body is composed of individual persons, and these also are particular subjects of rights.

6. The faithful are also divided into nations, provinces, municipalities, parishes, and special religious and pious societies, all of which are particular subjects of rights.

7. Every corporate body amongst the faithful is composed of individuals who are subjects of rights not only as human beings, or under some other rational quality, but as faithful members of the Catholic Church.

958. All these subjects of rights are inserted and incorporated into one another as members of a single body, composing the Church militant. Hence, all the rights of her members and of her organs (in so far as they are her organs) have their source in the Church considered as one simple body. The rights themselves are ordered and subordinated in the same way as the greater and lesser parts of the Church.

These parts, which receive their life from the unity of the Church, do not detract from this unity. In the same way, the various subjects of rights do not detract from the unity of the single subject of rights which is the entire body of the Catholic Church and her visible head. Local or personal obligations resulting from titles of common justice are, of course, always excepted.

959. Each of the subjects mentioned must be able to acquire all rights not incompatible with their state, provided there is a *just title* for doing so. But individuals can only acquire rights as

members of the faithful either in so far as they represent theocratic society (as trusted members) or in so far as the Church herself confers rights as necessary elements for their subsistence. In theocratic society, temporalities are never absolutely proper to individuals, strictly speaking, but always remain social benefits.

960. Finally, the titles of rights are often accidental facts. In this case, when the subjects of rights distinguished in theocratic society have an accidental fact as their title to rights, the rights themselves are accidental and occasional. Examples of such rights are those founded on grants of temporal jurisdiction made by the Church to rulers, or on donations. These rights are accidental, not essential to the Church, whoever their subject may be. There is no need to enlarge on this. Instead I offer a general conclusion to what has been said about Right in theocratic society.

CONCLUSION

961. A brief glance along the road travelled shows that we have proved:

1. All individuals sharing human nature possess in common the light of reason (being), that is, primitive, most universal truth. This fundamental good, which informs the human species, unifies individuals who are immovably intent on its essential illumination like bees around their queen. From this light springs equal right and equal obligation for all, together with identical moral virtue and an identical end, their eudaimonological good, the completion of such virtue. Consequently, the existence of a natural society of mankind cannot be denied as long as individuals know of one another's co-existence on earth. Such a society gives rise to the existence of *cosmopolitical Right*.[210]

---

[210] This is Kant's terminology; I would prefer to call it 'humanitarian Right'. But whatever the term, it seems to me a grave error, consonant with pagan society, to say (as Krug does, cf. *Aphorisms*, §48) that cosmopolitical

962. 2. When human beings use their common light of reason and come to see that our world must have a maker (and this is soon done as a result of stimulus from a kind of intellective instinct which permits no doubts),[211] they feel that their natural society *depends* upon the Creator (cf. *USR*, 109–114) in such a way that its *social ties* are conditioned by a *bond of seigniory* subjecting them to the first of all beings.

963. 3. If they come to see that the *being*, which shines in their minds and manifests all things, is the very same as that in God (although in God it is God, which is not the case in them), they arrive at the great realisation, reached by the outstanding minds of paganism, that man and God, in possession of a common good, form a common society. 'so that this whole world is to be considered as a city common to gods and men', as Cicero wrote.[212] However, the great pagan authors were unable to see that this was only a dim outline of the society God wished to form with human beings through Christ; it is not the perfection and completion of society.

964. 4. Universal, theocratic society is a sketch impressed in the essence of mankind by the Creator who, even after the disaster of the first sin, continued his masterly work through the saving truths revealed from time to time to men and women, and completed it once and for all when the Word took human flesh. Invisible, spirit-society, represented by a visible society called 'the Church militant', came to perfection; in a word, theocratic society, whose Right we have explained, began to exist on earth.

965 5. It is clear, therefore, that the universal Church cannot be confused with the natural society of mankind, just as a real house cannot be confused with the plans of the house. Nevertheless, the Church merits the title 'universal' because her first outlines have been sketched along with human nature. In fact, she invites all mankind to herself to bestow upon it the perfection of which it has some indetermined, unrealised idea to which

---

Right of any kind is only a part of State Right. Cosmopolitical Right is altogether independent of State Right which itself depends upon cosmopolitical Right.

[211] Cf. *CE*, 1264–1273.
[212] *De Legibus*, 1, 7.

it tends with its most secret, deepest desire, as to the fulfilment of its destiny.

966. 6. It is also clear that the nature of the perfect theocratic society, that is, of the Church, consists in its being a FAMILY SOCIETY IN THE SUPERNATURAL ORDER. It is not civil society, which has only the *modality of rights* as its object; the object and scope of theocratic society are human rights themselves in all their excellence as mankind's most precious good. It is a family society because it comes into existence by mode and title of *generation*, a reality by which one person communicates his own nature to another. This supernatural generation, the true origin of theocratic society, is the eternal generation of the Word, together with his Incarnation, followed by the incorporation and grafting of human beings in him. Through this mystical union, human beings share in the divine and human nature of Christ, and participate by adoption in his filiation. Through this society, therefore, the Creator became the father of human beings; the Church is simply God's family. In the Church there is *absolute,* but *not despotic* power, similar to that in the natural family.

The Church is also an invisible and visible society. As invisible, it is formed by the communication of God to human beings and, on the human side, by faith, love and obedience sworn to God. The visible aspect of the Church is the external expression and magisterium of this obedience and charity. The Church's external government is representative and delegated in its relationship to its invisible Ruler, but possesses its own authority relative to those it governs. The Church's end is twofold. From God's point of view, the end is his glory in the supreme happiness of the members; from the human point of view, the end is the glory of God through the greatest servitude that can be given, repaid by God with a relationship of utter friendship towards human beings. This unique society is based at one and the some time on supreme *seigniory, right* and *beneficence*, all of which reside united in the society's head who *desires* maximum servitude because this is in itself the greatest justice, and consequently brings the greatest happiness to those practising it. Maximum servitude given by the members is one with their supreme good: the essence of servitude and the essence of supreme social happiness are here a single essence.

[966]

Moreover, because this society is the highest and only true good, it is supreme amongst the societies of the faithful all of which must refer to it, and serve it. Just as lesser goods are not good unless referred to the supreme good, so societies are not upright but only sects and conspiracies unless they serve the supreme society, which alone renders other societies morally possible and just.

967. 7. It follows that the universal Church contains within itself the great organising principle of the human race. She is destined to bring together dispersed human beings, forming them into a single, ordered body. When mankind becomes a single flock with a single shepherd, 'according to the promises made by her Saviour and organiser' the work of creation will be complete, and the destiny of Adam's descendants will be achieved. All humanity will form the blissful city described by Zechariah: 'And Jerusalem shall be called THE CITY OF TRUTH.'[213] Eternal providence will have brought back mankind to its original design, and restored the family unity shattered by death, the effect of sin. If death had not entered the world as a punishment for sin, mankind springing from one father would never have been subject to division or separation. But when the original design failed, and its ruin provided the required opportunity, God remade it in greater splendour and beauty. He re-united human beings into a family once more, with himself, not Adam, as their father and true progenitor.

968. The concept of the theocratic society realised by the God-man is indeed exalted: all that can be said about it may be summed up in a single phrase: it is '*supernatural, domestic society*'. We have traced rather than developed the outline of its Right. Let us now continue by examining *natural, domestic society* [cf. *Rights in the Family*, vol. 5 of *The Philosophy of Right*], the noble symbol and, through Christ, the compendium, as it were, of theocratic society. When we have set out the right belonging to these two domestic societies in their respective supernatural and natural orders, we shall be able to unfold the more complicated right of civil society [cf. *ibid.*, vol. 6, *Rights in Civil Society*]. We need first to understand these two domestic

---

[213] Zech 8: 3.

societies which have *rights* and good as their aim and object, before examining and investigating civil society, whose aim and object is the *modality of rights*. We could not properly discuss the wise regulation of the modality of rights of the members of a society if the rights themselves with their social bonds and ties remained unknown.

Appendix

1. (488).

In speaking about the study of jurisprudence, Seneca remarks: 'I tell you: the wise person acts only after contemplating DIVINE and HUMAN things' (*Ep*). This opinion of the Stoics became an element of Roman law, which defined jurisprudence as 'the knowledge of divine and human things'. The great defect of Roman law, however, as I have often pointed out, lies in its incapacity for visualising Right outside the context of civil society. According to this view of things, civic Right is the basis of all other Rights, and thus a basis for tyrannising individuals. In modern times, it has become clear that human judges are incompetent in divine matters. Nevertheless, the initial mistake of the Romans, who developed the first treatises on natural Right as simple introductions to civil law (cf. *ER*, 31–48) has been perpetuated by German authors especially those of the critical school. Their insistence on the Roman concept of Right has outlawed from *rational Right* every jural relationship with the divinity. For them, Right concerns purely human beings. Such is the fundamental concept of Kant, for whom the principle of Right is found in the possibility of co-existence (cf. *ER*, 270).

As far as I can see, the science of Right is restored to its ancient dignity when reintegrated with the divine element abandoned in previous centuries. But, at the same time, I do not wish to encourage the revival of erroneous pagan jurisprudence. I simply want to consider rational Right in all its natural breadth, free of all arbitrary limits which make it a mere introduction to positive law in civil society. This society, like other particular societies, is restricted in so many ways (although even in civil society the magistrature should acknowledge theocratic Right at least to the extent of respecting, if not administering it). I am not at all sure that rational Right has yet been considered from a point of view enabling it to be seen without arbitrary limits, independent of and superior to positive human law. Samuel

Cocceji, for instance, in his treatise on natural Right, speaks on the one hand of the rights of the Creator, and sometimes rises above positive law when, for example, he classifies amongst opponents of Right those 'who say that rights were invented through fear of injustice, or who maintain, with Euphemius' (Thucyd., less. 6, c. 85, less. .5, c. 89) and others that right (civil right, that is) was instituted for private individuals, but is of no account amongst rulers for whom injustice is irrelevant' (*Dissert.* Proem. 12, less. 1, §40). But he contradicts himself by reducing everything to civic reality in accordance with his initial, declared intent of basing his system upon Roman law: 'This new system of natural law that I am expounding springs FROM ROMAN LAW ITSELF, which it is intended to illustrate' (*ibid.*, §1). Jean Domat is another example. Although a profoundly religious person, of considerable acumen, he made the same mistake as the Romans. His work on natural law serves only as a preface to a book entitled *LES LOIS CIVILES dans leur ordre naturel*. The error continues and contributes to past and present upheaval in France, where there will be no peace until the mistake is rectified.

2. (639).

These historians [who describe the very early history of individual nations] deal with the second cycle of human activity which begins with human degradation and rises to a certain cultural, moral and civil level. A description of the state of extreme barbarism from which these historians set out to follow mankind on its journey (and often overtake it in their imagination) may be found in Homer's passage on the Cyclops, in Euripides (*Cyclops*), in Cicero (*De Inventione*, bk. 1; and *Pro Sextio*), in Diodorus of Sicily (bk. 1, cc. 8, 43), in Lucretius (bk. 5), Horace (*Serm.*, bk. 1, Satyr. 3, and in *The Poetic Art*), in Manilius (bk. 1), and others. — Historians dealing with the first cycle, which begins with the good state of mankind and follows its successive degradation, are not to be found amongst the Greeks and the Romans. For this, we have to go to the East. Nevertheless, Greeks and Romans did possess confused traces of such ancient traditions in their descriptions of the golden age, and of the gods and heroes who preceded mere human beings on earth (cf. Lucretius, bk. 6; Virgil, *Georgics*, 2; Ovid, *Metamorph.*, 1; Oppianus, *Halieut.* bk. 2, v. 16 ss.). There is a particularly notable passage in Plato's *Timaeus*. The author says that the oldest recollections of the fires, volcanic eruptions and floods that swept over Greece had been lost. Greek histories were not very ancient, according to Plato, who mentions Solon's journey to Egypt and recounts what this legislator had heard from priests there:

> He said that he had asked the priests, who were all highly skilled in the matter, about the records of ancient times. He soon found that neither he nor any of the Greeks had the least knowledge of antiquity. Once he was amongst these priests and, by speaking about the ancient events of Athens, of the first Phoroneus, and of Niobe, as well as the flood which covered the world, of Pyrrha and of Deucalion and their posterity and the times in which each of these events took place, provoked them into talking about what interested them. At this point one of the oldest of them said: 'Solon, Solon, are you Greeks forever children? Is there not a single ancient in Greece?' When Solon asked him why he said this, the priest replied: 'Because your spirit is always young. You have received no ancient opinion from remote tradition, you have no grey-haired knowledge. This has happened because of the many different ways in which people have been and will be exterminated. Fire and flood have been the worst evils; but there have been many lesser ones. You have a story about Phaethon, the son of the Sun who mounted his father's chariot but was unable to follow his direction. Phaethon burnt up the earth and himself in the heavenly flames. Now although this seems only a story, there is a sense in which it is true. In fact, after a long period of time, the course of the heavens begins to decline and a conflagration bursts out. People who live on the heights where it is dry perish in far greater numbers than those who live near the sea and rivers. Now the Nile, which is useful to us in many ways also keeps away from us the plague of fire. Again when the gods of the waters wash away the dust of the earth under the great rains, the guardians who tend flocks of sheep and oxen on the high pastures escape this danger. But, your

cities, lying in the plain, are dragged into the sea by the force of the rivers. In our region, water never comes and never has come from on high. It rises up from the bowels of the earth…'

He goes on in this way to explain how memories of ancient times are preserved in Egypt and lost in Greece.

3. (688).

Socrates constantly pleads for light and consolation from some heavenly being. The need for a messenger from heaven to teach mankind is not, however, confined to Greek philosophers. The East testified to this need before the Greeks and longed for such a messenger. Christ is rightly called by the prophets the 'expectation of the nations'. I offer one quotation in confirmation of this. It is taken from Chung Yung, the second of the four sacred, classical books of China containing the teachings of Confucius. Chapter 31 speaks of the *perfectly holy man*, and describes him as 'one whose capacities are so extensive that he resembles an immense spring, bringing forth in due time all that is needed', and adds: 'His capacities are as vast as the heavens; the hidden spring from which they come is as deep as the abyss.' It continues:

> Let this perfectly holy man appear in all his virtue and powerful capacities, and the peoples of the world will pay him their homage; let him speak, and the peoples will believe his word; let him act, and the peoples will exult with joy… The fame of his virtue is like an ocean flooding the empire on all sides, and spreading north and south to barbarian lands. Travellers, merchants and artisans proclaim his fame to the ends of the earth; every living, breathing human being is ready to love and revere him. How true it is that his capacities and virtue are as high as heaven itself!

This ancient Chinese writer had already acknowledged that the longed-for person is the only true king. From the beginning of the chapter, he had written of the personage who formed the object of his desire:

In the whole universe, only the perfectly holy man, with
his capacity for complete knowledge and comprehension
of the essential laws of living beings, is worthy of sovereign
authority and power over human beings. His heart,
generous, affable and kind, enables him to benefit others
abundantly; noble, firm, tranquil and constant, it enables
him to provide for the reign of justice and right. His
capacity for decency, simplicity, seriousness, right and
justice attracts respect and veneration; his capacity for
procuring everything attainable by unremitting study, and
for enlightening the world by thorough investigation of
deep things and the most subtle principles, enables him
unfailingly to discern truth from falsehood, and good from
evil.

4. (861).

It is a universal law of mankind that rights without external
sanction are usurped by the strong. The condition of families
and individuals is explained in great part by this law, especially
the servile condition. History shows at every moment that the
strong form *civil society* to the exclusion of the weak, that is, of
those without sufficient influence or strength to overcome the
opposition of the strong who prevent their entrance into society. The persons thus constituting civil society and becoming
citizens greatly increase their power over the rejects, whose
rights have either insufficient guarantee or no guarantee at all.
This is the origin of *slavery*, and the reason why slaves were
soon considered mere things. If we look simply at the Middle
Ages, from which modern societies take their birth, we see that
force gradually gave way to Right through the hidden, con-
tinuous influence of Christianity. But how slowly progress was
made! In order to protect the rights of strangers in the midst of
powerful civil society, it was necessary: 1. for the strangers to
form part of society; 2. for them to acquire a level of influence
proportionate to the degree of their rights. The foundation of
municipalities was a great step ahead; a substantial number of
weak members obtained citizenship, and with it freedom. Their

influence in civil organisation, however, was disputed, often in bloody battles. The learned Ciberio says:

> The word 'bond-servant' vanished shortly after the formation of the municipalities. It was replaced by 'due-payers' because these people were obliged to pay dues to their masters. They were 'due-payers dependent on mercy' when the time and quantity of their duties was limited only by natural compassion, easily overcome by friendship. These unfortunates were also called 'mortmain' [dead hands] because they could not make wills or contracts, nor marry anyone who was not a bond-servant of the same master.
>
> (*Dell'economia politica del medio evo*, bk. 1, c. 2.)

If we examine the condition of the Church in recent times, we see that she has been deprived of the grade of civil influence required for sufficient defence of her temporal rights. She is no longer acknowledged civily as owner, and her goods have been considered as MORTMAIN, rather like the bond-servants called 'due-payers' and 'due-payers dependent on mercy', deprived of true ownership and incapable of making a will. The phrase has in fact been applied to clerics and religious, and shows the profound injustice of the thought behind it, as well as the impossibility of finding advocates for church temporalities in our modern civil society.

I am not considering all the causes which may have brought about this state of affairs. I am not denying that it can be seen as a reaction and compensation on the part of lay people; nor am I denying that clerics have often brought judgment upon themselves through their wrong interpretations of the Decretals: 'neither clerics nor monks should involve themselves in secular business' (*Decr. Greg.*, bk. 3, t. 50). But I am maintaining that greed and power have eliminated any civil influence on the part of the Church, and thus reduced it to the state of 'due-payers' at everyone's mercy. Julian the Apostate had already profited by the *moral counsels* of the Gospel to deprive Christians of their *rights*, and this sophism prevails once more. You love poverty, he said, because it is counselled by your Gospel; hence, I shall take your goods. You renounce the world because virtue is your aim; hence, I declare you unsuitable for any public office in the judiciary. You say that all your wisdom is to be found in the Crucified One whom you adore; hence, I forbid you education and so on. This is the same as saying that what a person does according to moral principles deprives him of his RIGHTS and gives others the possibility of usurping them. It is as though the spirit of the Gospel and church ministry were to exclude the good use of human things, rather than their abuse. But this has always been the pretext in such a sphere. It is at the basis of the odious French law which 'privileges' the clergy by excluding them from the peerage, or from sitting as deputies — rights which are common to all citizens. In 1778, at the German College in Rome, Benedetto Bonelli defended several excellent propositions against this attitude. His fifth proposition states:

> Churchmen are forbidden from undertaking the adminis-tration of secular business when their motive is greed; they are not forbidden to do so when their motive is charity and just and lawful precautions are in force.

In the appendix to his thesis (*De Ecclesiasticae vitae instituto a communis vitae societatisque officiis minime alieno*, sect. 1: 5), he affirms:

> Churchmen should not even take part in those occupa-tions in which envy may be their motive: guardianships, medicine, law and public offices. It is not the case that a churchman is always forbidden to act in secular business if it is privately or publicly necessary that he should do so (Thom., *ST*, II–II, q. 187, art. 2). So, if this work of theirs is not necessary, why should they do it? If it is necessary, let them do it. A person must be altogether a stranger to history if he is unaware that churchmen have carried out, when occasion demands, duties as guardians, executors and other officials in private and public. And in doing this they have acted for the sake of often bringing to society what is noble and salutary.

It is even more necessary for churchmen to be able to exercise the civil offices shown to be absolutely required for the defence of the Church.

5. (907).

'Every time Christians contract lawful marriage (that is, according to the formalities required by the Church), they form a sacrament'; 'the contracting partners are the ministers of this sacrament'. These two propositions are strictly interdependent. If the first is true, the second can easily be proved in the following way. The Council of Trent ruled that clandestine marriages carried out in preceding centuries were true and ratified marriages (*vera et rata matrimonia*) (Sess. 24, *De Reform.* c. 1. But the first proposition states that there is no true matrimonial contract between Christians without its being simultaneously a sacrament. Hence, the ministers of the sacrament are the contracting partners (the second proposition) because, as we said, they were truly married without the presence of a priest. It is necessary, of course, to prove the first proposition, that is, that there is no true, legitimate matrimonial contract between Christians without its being a sacrament. The argument runs as follows.

1. In church language, the phrase *vera et rata* refers only to sacramental marriages. But the Council of Trent has declared that marriages contracted without the presence of a priest are *vera et rata*. Therefore, these marriages are true sacraments.

Benedict XIV expresses the argument thus:

> The Fathers of the Council of Trent would never have said and declared that these marriages were TRUE AND RATIFIED unless they believed them to be true sacraments. This is Bellarmine's opinion (cit. c. 8) when he says that it was known to those most wise Fathers from the sacred canons, to which it is presumed they wished to conform in their language, that only those marriages are said to be TRUE AND RATIFIED which are sacraments of religion as well as civil contracts. We learn this especially from Innocent III (*De Divortiis*, c. 4), where he says: 'Although true marriage exists amongst the Gentiles, it is not ratified. It is true and ratified amongst the faithful because once the sacrament of faith has entered, it is never lost, but makes the sacrament of marriage ratified.'
>
> (*De Synod. D.*, bk. 8, c. 13: 5)

Benedict XIV adds to these words:

> Again if it comes about that marriage has been contracted
> secretly without the present of a priest, and that such a
> marriage is also a sacrament, it has to be admitted that THE
> CONTRACTING PARTIES THEMSELVES ARE THE MINISTERS,
> not the priest.
>
> (*Ibid.*)

2. There is no distinction in Scripture between lawful Christian marriage and the sacrament. The former is considered sacramental of its very nature. In fact, Christ establishes the *indissolubility* of Christian marriage, and excludes the possibility of other, dissoluble marriage. The indissolubility spoken about by Christ springs from the *sacramental bond*: 'What therefore God has joined, let not man put asunder' (Mt 19: 6). Marriage between Christians, therefore, is indissoluble not only by contract, but primarily by the law of God who prescribes the indissolubility of the contract itself. Hence, there is no true, Christian marriage which is not a sacrament.

3. When St. Paul says that Christian marriage *sacramentum est*, he includes all marriages between Christians without distinction, and hence acknowledges only sacramental marriage (Eph 5: 32). How does St. Paul prove that every Christian marriage is a sacrament? He shows that it represents the union between Christ and his Church. This union is represented according to the Apostle, in every marriage between Christians.

4. The Council of Trent speaks of only one possible *marriage* between Christians, which is simultaneously a *lawful contract* and a *sacrament* (sess. 24, *De Ref.*).

5. Innocent III, quoted above, shows that the contracting partners, as baptised members of the faithful, possess a certain *quality* through their indelible character which distinguishes their marriage from that of non-baptised people. The difference means that Christian marriage is true marriage, and *ratum*; marriage between non-baptised persons is true marriage, but not *ratum*. What does *ratum* mean? According to Innocent III, it means 'confirmed by the sacrament, which renders it indissoluble'. We should pay particular attention to the following words, especially these:

> It is true and RATIFIED amongst the faithful BECAUSE
> ONCE THE SACRAMENT OF FAITH HAS ENTERED, IT IS

NEVER LOST, but ratifies the sacrament of marriage.
(*De Synod. D.*, bk. 8, c. 13: 5)

6. Finally, Benedict XIV notes that in places where the Council has been promulgated, it could happen that a marriage comes about in the presence of the parish priest and two witnesses, without its being blessed — if, for instance, the bride and groom with two witnesses take the parish priest by surprise, and exchange their consent before him. If, as Cano says, the contract can be divided from the sacrament, so that such marriages would be contracts without the sacrament, the Church would not hesitate to say so:

> Lest the faithful who were living together in this way were to be perpetually deprived of the grace which the sacrament of marriage provides for those contracting marriage, the Church would have to compel, or at least exhort and induce them to legitimately renew their contract, using the sacred rites before the parish priest, by whose words the sacrament would come about. For the same reason, the Church would command clandestine marriages to be re-iterated before a priest, or would at least take care to establish them on a sound footing when they have been carried out in places where the decree of Trent has not been received. But in neither case do we see the renovation of marriage being urged by the Church. We may therefore conjecture without fear that each of the two contracts, although not marked by a priestly blessing, is indeed held by the Church as a sacrament.
>
> (*De Synod. D*, bk. 8, c. 13: 8)

We conclude that our opinion is not only the *most common*, as Lambertini says, but is that expressed by 'NEARLY ALL ancient theologians and interpreters of canon law' (*ibid*. Cf. also *Tertio saggio di observazioni sopra alcuni articoli del progetto di codice civile*, G. B. Monti, Mendrisio, 1836).

6. (931).

The right of nomination became hereditary when it was considered an entail on the ownership of a private chapel raised to the status of parish church. It was an abuse, however, from the start. The reasons inducing the Church to agree to it were the lack of priests, the intermingling of ecclesiastical and feudal power, and the decision of the kings of France to sequestrate church temporalities and enfeoff them to lay people (*Decret.* pt. 2, c. 16, q. 1, c. 59. *Capit.* 1, *Carol. Magni*, 803 AD, c. 1; *ibid.*, *Corr. Rom*). French royalty considered itself absolute patron of churches, and went so far as to interfere violently in the nominations to ecclesiastical offices. It usurped investiture to church posts, and exercised the same rights over priests as over its vassals (*Edict. Carol. M. ad comites*, 810 AD. — *Decret.* p. 2, c. 16, q. 7, c. 29 (Leo III, c. 800 AD); — c. 37, *eod.* (Council of Mainz. 813 AD); — c. 38, *eod.* (Council of Chalon-sur-Saône II, 813 AD). — *Capit.* I, *Carol. M.* 803 AD, c. 2, — *Capit. Ludov.* 816 AD, c. 9). In the 9th century, lay lords, despite the sanctions imposed by the Church, appointed priests at will. The following extract from the *De Privileg. et Iure Sacerdotum* of Agobard, Bishop of Lyons, will give some idea of the conditions of the time:

> The impious custom has grown to such an extent that you find almost no one alive, however little honour and temporal glory he may have achieved, who does not have his own domestic priest, not for the sake of obeying him but to demand from him unceasingly licit and illicit obedience not only in divine functions but even in human things. So you often find priests waiting at table, or mixing wines, or taking dogs for walks, or holding horses while ladies mount, or looking after tiny fields. The people of whom we are speaking cannot have good priests in their houses (what good cleric would degrade his name and life by bearing with such men?) NOR DO THEY CARE WHAT KIND OF CLERICS THEY ARE, OR HOW IGNORANT, OR HOW INVOLVED IN WRONG-DOING. All they want are their own priests so that they may have an excuse for abandoning the major churches and public devotions. It is clear that they do not keep priests for the honour of religion because they do not honour them. They nominate them contumeliously when they want us to ordain them priests. They ask or command us, saying: 'I have a cleric whom I have fed along with my own bond-servants, or beneficiaries, or paid servants,' or 'I have obtained him from someone or other, or

from one region or another. I want you to ordain him priest for me.' When this has been done, they think that senior priests are unnecessary for them, and they frequently abandon public devotions and sermons.

(De privileg. et jure sacerdot., c. 3)

Bishops and Councils, especially the 3rd and 4th Lateran Councils, tried to remedy the damage, but only to the extent of maintaining that the local bishop was judge of the suitability of priests nominated by patrons. The hereditary right of nomination was left unmolested for the sake of avoiding greater evils (Council of Seligenstadt, 1022 AD, c. 13 — Council of Bourges, 1031 AD, c. 21. — *Decretal.*, bk. 3, t. 5, *De praebend.,* c. 3 — *De jure patron.*, c. 4: 33 — bk. 5, t. 37, *De poen.,* c. 11).

Index of Biblical References

Numbers in roman indicate paragraphs; numbers in italic indicate footnotes. Bible references are from RSV (Common Bible) unless marked †. In these cases, where the author's use of Scripture is dependent solely upon the Vulgate, the Douai version is used.

Index of Persons

Numbers in roman indicate paragraphs or, where stated, the appendix (app.); numbers in italic indicate footnotes.

General Index

*Numbers in roman indicate paragraphs or, where stated, the appendix (app.);
numbers in italic indicate footnotes*

right and, 490

Government
as competent judge, 935
despotic, *7*

Government of Church
defence of right and, 779
God's power *de jure* and *de facto*,
  736–744
laws and, 935
ministers of, 731
seven ways of, 748–755

Grace (divine)
communication of God, 696
human beings and, 707
light of, 677
order of, 606
perception of divinity, 707, 713
revelation and, 693
theocratic society and, 694–697

Happiness
Church and, 758, 768, 771, 776
foundation of all rights, 770
God and human, 553, 563–567, 721,
  966
good and, 641, 648
human good and, 641–643, 645, 663
intelligent beings and, 650
love and, 648
supreme value of, 867
virtue and, 647

Harems
women and, 506

Heaven
God and, 554

Hell
Christ and, 631
God and, 554, 605

Heretics
priesthood and, *185*
punishment of, 820–821

Hierarchy
visible government of Church, 731

Holiness
Christ and, 625, 626, 629, 725

Church and, 725
creatures and, 553, 725
doctrine of, 615
God and, 562–565, 590, 595, 691, 694,
  725

Holy Orders
aggregation and, 748
divine sacrifice and, 749

Human Beings
Christ and, 630–631, 705–709
Church and, 758
end of, 565–566
God and, 539, 576, 690, 698, 711
good and, 576, 684
happiness and holiness of, 563–567
ideal being and, 683–685
love of, 645
right and 521–525
three goods in, 641–650
truth and, 645, 683, 690
virtue and, 690

Human Nature
Incarnation and, 701, 704
unity of, 649

Idea
contemplation of ideas, 686
distinction between God and,
  672–675; *85*
human species and, 645
love and, 645
truth and, 645, 672

Ideal Being
beauty and lovableness of, 685
common good, 693, 695
essence and, 683
God and, 550–551, 574, 588, 673, 682,
  685, 963
intellect and, 574
knowledge and, 683–684
love of, 683
moral good and, 683
natural things and, 684
order of finite beings and, 684–685
power of, 689
real being and, 682, 685
theocratic society and, 682
truth and, 682

in fact, 739, 745
liturgical, 749, 755
of binding and losing, 751, 755
of instruction, 779
of organisation, 754–755
of teaching, 753, 755, 779
ordinative, 779
seven forms of, 747, 755, 790, 804,
807, 894

Priesthood
of faithful, 891–894, 896, 899
public, ministerial, 894, 900; *184*

Primacy of Peter
Christ and, 758

Principle
ontological law of, 576

Protestantism
territorial system of, *191*
use of word 'Church', 913

Purgatory
Church in, 732

Rationalism
elimination of, 675

Reason
Christ as, 615
existence of God and, 687
light and, 615–616
theocratic society and, 681
see also **Light (of Reason)**

Reconciliation, *see* **Penance**

Religion
natural, 687
right and, 488 ss.
scientific method and, 519–
use of word, *190*

Resentment, Jural
baptised persons and, 866
rights and, 866

Revelation
grace and, 693–694
theocratic society and, 691–694

Right
activity and, 493–495
civil, *70*
civil power and science of, 862
contingent and necessary facts and,
532
cosmopolitical, 961
damage to, 571
derived rational, 532, 534
exercise of, 773
God's dominion as, 569–572
human beings and, 521–525
peace and, 853
positive, 526–529
rational, 520 ss.; *app.* no. 1
religion and, 488 ss.
special, 524–525
State, *210*
supernatural, 788, 862
to absolute freedom, 785–787
to recognition, 780
universal, 477–481
see also **Communal Right, Rights**

Rights
God and real, 532
mankind and, *app.* no. 4
of Church, 854
of everyone relative to Church,
800–803
publicists and imperfect, 954
supreme goods and, 659
see also **Modality of Rights, Right**

Roman Law
jurisprudence in, *app.* no. 1
right in, *app.* no. 1

Sacraments (in general)
matter of, *187*

Sacrifice
defined, *56*
faithful and, 897–900
God's own, 749
theocratic power and, 749, 755

Sanction (ecclesiastical)
civil sanction and, 822
deprivation as, 814, 816
excommunication as, 816
force of, 810–813, 818–819
imposition of penance as, 814–815, 817

punishments as, 815–822; *137*
right of, 807–822

Scientific Method
religion and, 519–534

Seigniory of God
absolute, 538–539
admission to Church and, 879
beneficence of, 579–585, 710–712
inalienability of, 586
ministers of, 608–610
naturalness of, 575–578, 962
nature of, 546–568
propogation of Church and, 797
reasonableness of, 573–574
right of, 569–572
theocractic society and, 536 ss.; 966
three marks of, 573–585
uniqueness of, 536–537
see also **Dominion of Christ, Servitude to God**

Servants
domestic society and, *5*
rights denied to, 511

Servitude to God
Christ and, 620–621
human beings and, 581
necessary and free, 605
obligation of, 584
of faithful and unfaithful, 623–624
one only, 540–545
tendency of, 578
three acts of, 587–602
see also **Seigniory of God**

Sick, Sacrament of, *see* **Extreme Unction**

Sin
death and, 967

Slavery
abolition of, 868, 870
civil government and abolition of, 869
England and abolition of, 868
origin of, *app.* no. 4
see also **Slaves**

Slaves
rights denied to, 511

societies formed by, 870
see also **Slavery**

Society
common good of, 641, 644, 655
communion of good, 644, 655–657, 679, 690
competent judge in, 935
consent and, 707
constitutive elements of, 679
dismissal from, 883
divine, 491
intimacy of, 655, 656
mankind and, 483–485
mankind and theocratic, 486 ss.
material goods and, 826
ownership and, 824–825, 827
possessions and end of, 826–827
right and, 479–483
see also **Civil Society, Domestic Society, Natural Universal Society, Particular Societies, Theocratic Society**

Sovereign Pontiff
choosing pastors, 923
church discipline and, 918
church temporalities and, *203*

Subject
object and, *54*

Supernatural Order
Church and, 966
God and, 674, 676–678
real form and, 674
theocratic society and, 678

Theocratic Society
beneficence and, 966
Christ and, 705–709
Christian Church and, 671 ss.; 964
common good and, 679–687, 693
communion in good and, 689, 687–690, 692
defined, 669
dominion of God and, 710–712
glory and, 714–715
governmental right in, 736 ss.
grace and, 694–697
Incarnation and, 698–703, 964, 966
kingdom of God, 711
levels of perfection of, 679–703